ADVANCE PRAISE

"Oh, how I wish I had read this book when I was raising my spirited child all those years ago! In her book, *Being Happy, Raising Happy,* Maureen Lake shares her personal journey of raising a child with a combination of learning, emotional, and social challenges. But this isn't just a book about how to parent a challenging child. It is a book about how helping yourself can strengthen your whole family."

"Maureen bravely shares the impact of her parenting efforts on her own mental and physical health as well as the tensions on the family as a whole. I recognized in her the feeling felt by many parents, but particularly by those who raise children who struggle to find success in school, to form long-term friendships, and to gain the problem-solving and decision-making skills needed to feel contented in life. Maureen conveys so well how attention to yourself is the foundation of being a good parent. Feeding your own needs helps you meet their needs. I must say the book has inspired me want to pass on her wisdom to other parents."

Toni Linder
Professor Emerita
Morgridge College of Education
University of Denver

"A child is like a butterfly in the wind. Some can fly higher than others, but each one flies the best it can. Why compare one against the other? Each one is *different*. Each one is *special*. Each one is *beautiful*. Maureen shares her wisdom, compassion, and strength as she opens up and expresses ways to reduce stress and anxiety whilst creating a closer relationship with one's spirited child. Her tips, tactics, and approaches provide every individual a path to grow and learn new ways to adapt and change one's journey through life while helping both your child and yourself find your wings."

Lynn Kuhn, M.A., CCC-SLP
Language-Literacy Links Consultant
Board of Directors of the International Dyslexia
Association-Rocky Mountain Branch

"With insight, vulnerability, and passion, the author takes us on a journey – one that many parents of kids with complex struggles know all too well. Ultimately the author leads us to the connection between our own self-care as a parent and person and the well-being of our child. With concrete and useful tools about such important topics as the relationship between stress and food and the value in reducing stress with mindfulness techniques, the author draws a path towards greater self-care, reduction of stress and cortisone levels, and greater happiness. As a psychotherapist, I know this path quite well. I will *highly* recommend this book to my patients. As a parent I was touched by the author's self-disclosure and vulnerability, and greatly valued the knowledge I gained in reading this book. Maureen Lake has given gifts of love and knowledge to her daughter, to herself, and now to us."

Bradley Lake, LICSW, LCSW-C

"Upon reading the first few pages, I was totally hooked. I felt like Maureen was sitting across the table teaching me the importance of taking care of myself, and how my wellness will positively impact my child. My child is highly sensitive and this book reminded me to be more aware of how my emotions affect her."

Gretchen Burman
The Adventures of Ooga and Zeeta
www.character-u.com

BEING HAPPY
RAISING
HAPPY

The Empowered Mom's Guide to
Helping Her Spirited Child Bloom

MAUREEN LAKE

NEW YORK

LONDON • NASHVILLE • MELBOURNE • VANCOUVER

BEING HAPPY, RAISING HAPPY

Published in New York, New York, by Morgan James Publishing in partnership with Difference Press.
www.MorganJamesPublishing.com

The Morgan James Speakers Group can bring authors to your live event. For more information or to book an event visit The Morgan James Speakers Group at
www.TheMorganJamesSpeakersGroup.com.

ISBN 978-1-68350-693-5 paperback
ISBN 978-1-68350-694-2 eBook
Library of Congress Control Number: 2017911979

Cover & Interior Design by:
Megan Whitney
Creative Ninja Designs
megan@creativeninjadesigns.com

In an effort to support local communities, raise awareness and funds, Morgan James Publishing donates a percentage of all book sales for the life of each book to Habitat for Humanity Peninsula and Greater Williamsburg.

Get involved today! Visit
www.MorganJamesBuilds.com

This book is dedicated to my beautiful and determined daughter Devin. Her ability to fight against all odds has taught me more about life, love, and resilience than I could ever have imagined. Without her this book would not have been written. Her journey is my ray of light and hope for tomorrow.

CONTENT

FOREWORD

How do you systematically short-circuit a child's confidence?

Easy.

Put them in an environment that doesn't make sense. Or, make them play a game they're not wired to play.

That was me....

I grew up with undiagnosed dyslexia until I was 20. It wasn't until a freak car accident caused me to get psychological tests done that I found out I had dyslexia.

It was a relief.

I finally found out why I had this internal struggle going on of why or how some kids could understand things I couldn't....

I finally found out why it took me four days of reading, eight hours a day, to finiash a small book for a school report....

And, I finally found out school wasn't built to feed me confidence. Which was why I rebelled against it as much as I could.

Give me P.E. class, recess, or experiments, and my brain and body would light up. Ask me to sit and read, and all I wanted to do was joke around and continue to play the "class clown."

After years of being forced through a routine you're not suited to thrive in, your self-esteem can get trampled on. Mine did. Yet, there are powerful forces a dyslexic or anyone with a "learning disability" has that begin working for them: resiliency and imagination.

Think about it: If the world you're living in isn't built for your wiring, you develop a resiliency to overcome. And, you develop an imagination that helps you find new ways to figure it out, because if you don't, nobody else will. And when you think of the qualities you need to win at life, resiliency and imagination are at the top of the list.

A recent study found dyslexics, (or people with other "learning disabilities") have a high likelihood of becoming entrepreneurs.

That's me.

I've started a lot of businesses. Some worked. Some didn't. But through it all, I kept going, because I learned at a young age that was my only choice.

The danger with all these labels society likes to place on people, is thinking it's a "defect."

It's not.

I happen to think it's an "infect." Meaning, it infects you with a superpower only you are uniquely qualified to handle.

I've gone through bouts of depression in my life and without that "hardening of the will" I developed when I was younger, I don't know if I could've come out the other side. Throughout, my younger years, I was lucky to have patiently firm parents to help move me forward.

And when you take the advice and perspective Maureen Lake has laid out in this book, you have no idea the immeasurable impact you could make on your son or daughter. The fact you're even reading this book shows you have a desire to be a powerful force in your child's life. Even if you grab three ideas from the next few chapters, those are three dominos you're dropping that could have immeasurable results.

Take it from a kid that went through most of what's in this book: being a parent who understands your kid's world is the greatest gift you could give.

Todd Herman
Entrepreneur/Dad/Unstoppable Dyslexic

INTRODUCTION

*"Every flower must push through
the dirt to get to bathe in sunlight."*

JUDA SALMELA

The tears poured out of my eyes as I tried not to sob in front of my two boys. I worked hard to catch my breath, knowing if I didn't concentrate intensely I would give in to the sadness and start to cry. Once again I felt powerless and confused.

Why did this continue to happen over and over again? Later, I would feel guilty and alone in my grief, and my two confused adult sons would be helplessly wondering what they could do to make things better.

It's always been like this, ever since my daughter was a little curly-haired bundle of emotions. At first I honestly thought it was just that she had a more challenging temperament than my two calm boys; I'd listened to every stereotype about girls being more emotional and volatile. Even so, everything was different with her from the moment of conception.

I knew she was a girl, even though I didn't know her sex while I was pregnant. I used to joke that "only a daughter could make a mother feel this sick." Little did I know at the time that this beautiful daughter of mine would teach me to see a staggering array of emotions I'd never truly experienced before, feelings that taught me how to parent, love, and eventually self-care.

Raising a child with emotional outbursts and somewhat ridiculous reactions to minute situations was challenging and worrisome. As she grew, so did her ups and downs as well as my concerns. She was diagnosed early on with dyslexia, but since I have a masters in early childhood special education, I knew there was more going on than that, and that this was just the beginning of our journey.

My son had been formally diagnosed with dyslexia two years prior, and it's not uncommon for this unique learning challenge to run in families. As a special education teacher of many years, I'd befriended moms from various walks of life who had children with severe needs ranging from autism to dyslexia.

I knew in my gut that there was more to my daughter's picture than what she currently presented.

Later came the diagnoses of ADHD and depression, joining with dyslexia to form "the big trifecta" or a "triple whammy," as we called it when I taught special education. I knew from my professional experience that the road ahead would not be easy for my lovely, innocent child. Sure enough, there came a time, later, when my precious daughter began self-medicating with food and alcohol.

I worried about her health and her survival.

The school years were challenging. Making friends was agonizing, and she was in distress more often than not. I went to bed most nights wondering if she would be alive in the morning. In retrospect, the professionals trying to help were grasping at straws; she didn't fit into a neatly wrapped package. Truthfully, my daughter was three gifts wrapped into one amazing, whimsical, and challenging ensemble.

Each year brought unfamiliar and perplexing obstacles. I strove to find new ways to educate myself and to help her cope while, drenched with guilt and embarrassment, I kept my stress and anxiety hidden from others. Family time either began or ended in an emotional tizzy that left me feeling angry, alone, and completely inadequate as a mother.

I worried about everything when it came to my daughter. I obsessed about her future and if she would graduate high school, let alone college like her brothers. Would she even be able to hold down a job as an adult? Why was she so unhappy, practically from birth?

Was I somehow directly responsible for her struggles?

As I lost sleep, I lost myself, and the stress and strain I felt were unbearable. How could I be a source of support for my daughter when I could barely support myself? What could I do to improve my situation so I could better cope with hers?

My never-ending story took a left turn as I began searching for answers to a whole new set of questions. I knew in the deepest reaches of my soul that there had to be more knowledge available than there had been even a few years before.

Google was my new best friend as I started to search all sorts of terms, including dyslexia, anxiety disorders, stress management techniques, brain development, and nutrition. Imagine my surprise when I learned, many years after my daughter's initial diagnosis, that thanks to innovations in technology, science, and integrated medicine, a new array of opportunities had opened up for my daughter.

As a truth seeker, I have a never-ending desire to obtain knowledge. My route to becoming a certified holistic health coach was evident to me once I understood the undeniable connection between good nutrition and well-being. I was on a mission to change the trajectory of my family's old path to a new direction that included health and wellness, scientific research, and mindfulness. What I'm sharing with you isn't rocket science, but I know from experience that taking the first steps to managing stress and anxiety might as well be.

It's not easy to realize that your tension, nervousness, and distress directly impact your child. I kept it very well hidden. I laughed and smiled at all the right times, and from the outside it looked like I was happy. Truthfully, my immediate family didn't even know the level of hurt I lived with every day. By hiding my sadness, I thought it might go away, but it didn't. It took getting physically sick to understand the depth of what stress can and will do to your health over time. I wish I'd known what I know now back when my child was younger. It's impossible to know for sure if our outcomes would have been any different, but I'd like to think so.

Many fantastic and profound changes have come about in my daughter's life since applying this newfound knowledge, including being able to reduce her medication, seeing positive results from dietary changes, and her finding her spirit. The scariest part was starting. It's understandable that the first step can be the most difficult to take, but once you do, you will find that new, life-changing ideas and transformations await you and your child.

How did I reduce my distress and help transform my child? The areas that I focused on are in the chapters that follow. But, as I mentioned before, my story is never-ending, and so is my daughter's. As she transforms, I do, too. As I manage my self-care, it directly impacts and influences her self-care.

I'm a healthier, more complete person because of my daughter and what she has allowed me to learn from her growth process. Now, I want to share these areas of focus with you in the hope that they will help you, too, reduce your anxiety while allowing your spirited child to bloom.

All five chapters are chock full of ideas and suggestions on how to reduce cortisol levels in your system (the deadly stress hormone). Walking down the path to wellness means you will discover an overall stress reduction in your body and mind.

The lifestyle changes that will occur as you delve into the areas of nutrition, mindfulness, relationships, sleep, and healing will absolutely increase your sense of well-being and contentment.

These five areas are simple yet proven methods to lower your stress, anxiety, and depression. The research is clear, and the benefits are amazing. Each topic takes into account the function of your brain, the increased cortisol levels in your body, and how best to change and reduce these levels for optimal health and well-being.

The first step, and often the most difficult to take, is to promise yourself that you're worth this time and energy. I know only too well that you put yourself second, even third – no, probably last in the hierarchy of need.

You are the forgotten one, but the one that most often needs the most because you give the most. Take a chance on yourself and your self-care. It will impact not only you, but also the health of your family and child. Listen to your heart, and take a chance on this healthy journey toward wellness.

CHAPTER 2
HIDING

*"Raise your words, not your voice. It is rain
that grows a flower, not thunder."*

RUMI

A few years into your child's elementary school career, you start to pick up on subtle signs from other parents. You hear through the grapevine about birthday parties your child wasn't invited to, or can't comprehend why only five kids attended your child's party when you asked the entire class.

Slowly, parents who were your so-called "friends" are now separating themselves from you. The teacher called to share that your child lashed out at another kid on the playground, and then you find out that it was unprovoked. Your go-to babysitter is suddenly making up some creative reasons as to why she can't babysit anymore (seriously, she's going to the Bahamas for the weekend?).

You're as sad and lonely as your child is, mirroring her feelings of rejection and the effects of bullying on her.

Probably the most alarming thing right now is the unpredictable behavior at home. The temper tantrums, arguments, and lashing out are suddenly crueler and more frequent. Your child is crying, unhappy, and moody. Without warning, she suddenly and frequently starts having night terrors that keep her awake at night.

Eventually, your other children prefer hanging out at a friend's house and rarely do they have friends over anymore. This is crazy! Your house used to be the coolest place in the neighborhood, and now it's empty? It seems like the older your child gets, the more she morphs into another person who you have to figure out from scratch. Two steps forward, three steps back, over and over again.

Spirited children come in all shapes and sizes, with various idiosyncrasies, incredible energy, and fabulous gifts. Some kids appear to be hard-wired to disrupt the peace for no real reason, while other children receive a label early on in their development.

Immediately after hearing my daughter's diagnosis of dyslexia, ADHD, and depression, my husband suddenly stopped dead in his tracks to cry in the parking lot, out of sight and sound of others, trying to digest the knowledge that something important was "wrong" with his child.

Fear of and anxiety over the unknown made things feel scary and unpredictable. Naming a problem can help us understand the situation – and if you're like me, you've been researching every book available on dyslexia, ADHD, and depression.

I know it helps a bit with reducing some built-up anxiety, allowing you to feel that the label is legitimate and researched.

Truthfully, the diagnosis is less important than the support and resilience you need during these upcoming trying times. But maybe by burying yourself in research, you're trying to hide in plain sight. I understand, because I used to hide, too.

Raising a spirited, even challenging child can be gut-wrenching, isolating, and lonely. It can also be uplifting, hopeful, and incredibly gratifying. Sometimes you feel like you're the only one who is fighting for your child, and the only person on earth who truthfully understands her. Even so, you find your child similar to a hurricane, changing unpredictably with the wind.

You've done the research, read every book you can get your hands on, and are still bewildered. You've tried a jillion different behavior interventions and parenting techniques; you could teach a weeklong retreat on the topic and still need extra days to share what you've learned.

You keep most of the embarrassing situations and conversations close to the vest, because if you don't talk about it, it just might go away or at the very least stay hidden in clear sight. That's what I did too, but it left me isolated and vacant during the most trying days of my life.

Your child is distressed, and so are you. To help your child, it's critical to get your own care under control. So what about you? How are you holding up? It's no wonder you sometimes feel your heart racing when you're literally standing still. The everyday routines and habits that were so natural are now challenging and strenuous because your diet, health, relationships, alone time, and sleep are all discombobulated.

Did you know the racing heart, the panic attacks, and the feeling that you've got to run away are all due to cortisol raging through your system and causing chronic stress, anxiety, and eventually depression?

Stress, Anxiety, and Depression

You've heard the stories before; a baby is trapped under a car, and somehow a mother lifts the car up to rescue her child. Or a house is on fire, and the father runs into a burning building to save his family. This stress is known as "fight or flight," and it can be helpful in certain situations. It's acute, but it's out of your system within 90 minutes.

Chronic stress, on the other hand, the kind of stress you feel every day, takes a toll on your health and well-being. You have a tendency to ignore it, hoping it'll diminish, but this is the type of stress that affects your health, your body, and your immune system.

And, unfortunately, there is also distress, the kind of stress that occurs when something unthinkable happens, such as divorce, financial or work difficulties, or death of a loved one.

The kind of stress we will explore together is chronic stress, the ongoing grind that occurs to your system, day in and day out, sometimes without you even knowing it's happening.

This type of stress sucks us dry; it's the kind of stress that makes us snap at our husband and yell at our kids. It keeps us awake at night and causes that tummy spread that's suddenly increasing out of nowhere.

We've known for years that chronic stress makes us more susceptible to disease, and now we know that it ages us as well. Stress actually eats away at our telomeres, the end points of our DNA, making us sick and aging us before our time.

The Nitty Gritty Impact on Your Health

Public enemy number one is cortisol. Poor little cortisol, it means well but certainly doesn't know when to quit. When you experience constant stress, it doesn't know how to turn itself off, so the stress hormone is churning in your system and causing all sorts of horror stories.

When cortisol spikes, it sends a message to your brain to eat something sweet or high in carbs to satisfy the survival tactic built into your DNA (think flight or fight). That's why, when you're fretting over your child's latest incident and everything else that's happened over the past month, emotional eating takes over (hence the tummy spread). With cortisol levels raging through your system, and causing glucose spikes and other consequences, your body and brain will suffer in three significant ways.

First, your immune system takes a beating. Are you getting more frequent colds or are your allergies kicking in, even when it's not full-blown allergy season? There is a direct relationship between your nervous system, endocrine system, and immune system. It's a well-known fact that chronic stress suppresses your immune system.

Second, your heart takes a shellacking with chronic stress too. All the stress hormones and biological changes that occur also impact your heart rate and blood pressure. The racing heart or palpitations you feel are directly related to the level of stress and cortisol racing through your system. Chronic stress leads to high blood pressure, hardening of the arteries, an enlarged heart, heart attack, or heart failure. Cortisol has a powerful impact on your body, all because of the stress you undergo every day.

Finally, stress wreaks havoc on your digestive system, because with chronic stress, normal digestion doesn't occur. Your small intestine slows down and your large intestine ramps up, causing diarrhea, constipation, or both. If you have irritable bowel syndrome, colitis, or Crohn's disease, you are probably very aware of the impact that chronic stress has on your gut.

Prolonged stress will also throw off your digestive system's balance of good and bad bacteria, and change the chemical environment of your stomach, leading to leaky gut. Luckily, there are ways to cut the cortisol level in your system and manage your stress and anxiety on a daily basis.

That is why I wrote this book for you. I don't want you to have to suffer years of abuse within your body when you can begin the healing process right now. We can fix you up with a little bit of support and guidance. The dual benefit is not only improved health for you but also renewed physical and emotional resilience to help reduce the effects of stress on you, your child, and your family.

How Your Stress Affects Your Child

We've established that parenting a child through their emotional roller coaster isn't easy. Sometimes your child's issues will trigger memories of an earlier experience – or even trauma you may have experienced yourself as a child. These can be hard to let go, but the one thing that is crystal clear is that you are a role model for your child.

Your fears and anxieties about your life will have an effect on your child's self-esteem and confidence level. Your sweet child is watching you and observing how you handle certain situations. You're laying the groundwork for how they will handle similar situations.

Let's be honest. You are the essence of your child's social and emotional development. They will learn from you how best to manage and cope even when they may have problems regulating these areas consistently. Also, the choices you make while reacting to them can diffuse or elevate a situation, and possibly send your child into a downward spiral.

You can assuage your child's anxiety just by making acceptable choices for yourself. Choose now to be a great role model for your child. All it takes is for you to become aware and open to trying new behaviors that will create lifelong changes for you.

The transformations addressed in this book will change your DNA, change your child, and change your family. Yes. You are that powerful!

For each of the five key chapters in this book, I've provided a short quiz. Use your results to figure out which areas are important for you to focus on to reduce your stress levels.

We are knowledge seekers, you and me, so be prepared to take a journey and learn about what makes your stress go into overdrive, and understand how you can slow down and make lasting, lifelong positive changes that will benefit not only you but also your child. Inspiration, compassion, and strength are what will get you through this journey. Explore the five ways I transformed my life, and, in the process, bettered my child's life, too.

CHAPTER 3
STRENGTH

"Life is the flower for which love is the honey."

VICTOR HUGO

A few years ago Alex and her mom Linda came into my special education room for a quick debrief after Alex's annual Individual Education Plan (IEP) meeting. Alex, a loving nine-year-old with curly brown hair, sat quietly at the table with a solemn look on her face. This expression was a common one for Alex; she rarely smiled or laughed when I worked with her during the week, although her eyes would light up when I let her do her school work with colored pens and pencils. After a lingering hug goodbye, she went off to recess with her class, and I had some time to chat with Linda about her spirited child.

Listening, I came to understand the difficulties Alex had with friends and family, which mirrored her tension and anxiety at school. It was evident how painful this was for her mom; Linda's eyes welled up with tears as we talked.

Linda told me that Alex threw tantrums almost daily, especially when she had to go to school. Often Alex got to school long after the bell rang because of all the time it took to get her out the front door. On top of that, many days Alex would come home from school early because the nurse would call and ask for her to be picked up immediately for either a stomach ache or a headache. Linda said she was thankful she was a stay-at-home mom; otherwise, she would have had to quit her job. Her anguish was apparent in her posture, her voice, and her demeanor.

Every day, Linda explained, she encountered new challenges with Alex. Linda shared that she spent too much time worrying about her daughter. From the minute Alex left for school, until she came home in the afternoon, Linda stewed over her daughter's well-being. She was overwhelmed by the idea that Alex was miserable all day and wondered if her daughter was learning anything at all since she hated school so much.

Linda was starting to wonder if her stress and anxiety were impacting her health and her relationship with her husband. There were days she stopped at McDonald's each and every morning for a Diet Coke and not one, but two Egg McMuffins with sausage. Gone were the days when she would drink a smoothie in the morning and then take the dog for a long walk.

Linda shared that she read all the time, trying to figure out what in the world was wrong with her child, but that it only made her more anxious about Alex's future because she couldn't find specific answers to her questions. Most days, Linda was angry and frustrated; no one appeared to understand the struggle she was going through with her daughter, day in and day out.

Linda's sisters thought she had it made, living in a lovely home with four beautiful children. But most of her family lived hundreds of miles away, and honestly, they didn't want to hear about her difficulties, mainly because they had problems of their own.

Linda's husband was busy working all the time and came home most nights after dinner, when the most difficult period of the day with Alex had passed. Most evenings, Linda was so tired and stressed she could barely muster a smile, let alone any intimacy. When her husband walked through the door, she often wondered to herself, "Is he really working late every day?" She hated herself for being suspicious of him, because after all, he provided the family with a beautiful house, great vacations, and status-seeking cars.

From the outside, everything looked great because Linda worked hard on the façade, but on the inside, Linda was crying for help, lonely, and hiding in her misery. She wondered out loud what happened to her laid back, comfortable, and lively parenting style?

Although Linda told me she was beginning to understand that when you have a child who is anxious and distressed, your parenting style must change to accommodate this, she also knew her coping skills had degraded over time. While she was in nurture and protection mode with Alex, her inner self was in constant turmoil. She didn't know how to break the vicious cycle.

My heart broke for her when she explained that she didn't know how to find her old self; she didn't even understand where to look. At that point, we were both tearing up, cramped and curled over from sitting on kid-size chairs in my resource room.

Linda said that constant chronic stress was taking a toll on everyone and everything: on her, her children, and her precarious marriage. She was at a crossroads, and felt she needed to figure out a way to change her life. I saw a vacant stare in her eyes as she slowly looked up and said, "I think I'm lost."

Do You Want to Know a Secret?

I think we can all relate to Linda in most ways; I know I can. It seems like only a blink of an eye ago when I was worrying and obsessing over my daughter – actually, I still worry, and that will never change by virtue of being a parent.

It destroyed me to know my daughter didn't have many friends and that the cool kids were bullying her and making fun of her behind her back on the soccer field. As I distanced myself from the moms of these children, I often wondered if I was too sensitive and questioned if I should have somehow intervened.

I didn't confront anyone and sought the haven in my home, blaming others and feeling a sense of shame and guilt. In retrospect, my nervousness and apprehension only added to my daughter's insecurity. I was reflecting my unhappiness onto my daughter, and she was soaking it up like a sponge.

Reflecting back on these terribly upsetting memories, I realize it was a process to get to where I am today – and trust me, it didn't happen overnight. It started with talking to what seemed like hundreds of parents who were experiencing very similar life-impacting changes because of their child.

The consensus is the same no matter what the child's diagnosis: moms are suffering. The stress and anxiety of raising a "spirited" child are life-changing in many ways, good and not-so-good, but the bottom line is that it can rob a mom of her health and well-being because, let's face it, our needs are the last to be met. Period.

All Alone

Waking up many times a night takes a toll. It sucks you dry in so many horrific ways, from your pores to your psyche. I not only didn't sleep consistently, but I woke up in a panic situation more than once, dripping in sweat and wondering if I'd had a heart attack.

When you don't deal with your stress, you will pay the price. It might take years to reach your personal threshold and tip over into illness, but whatever yours is, reach it you will if you don't do something about it first.

It didn't take long, considering the worry and frustration that had become a routine part of my daily grind, to find myself at the doctor's office suffering from panic attacks and high blood pressure.

I was far from overweight, but there is a history of high blood pressure in my family and my sister, only two years older than I, had suffered a stroke at a young age. I took this wake-up call seriously, so I diligently took my meds. But that was all I did, and so the stress and anxiety continued, as did the panic.

I had constant headaches and, suddenly, a pooch around my tummy. Wondering where in the heck that came from, my OBGYN mentioned that stress eating could be the culprit. Truth be told, I was eating a lot of sweets every day.

This was after I had to have a hysterectomy because of unbearable endometriosis, which later I found could also be caused by stress! At 40 years old, I felt and looked so much older. I was obsessed with everything except myself, and I was emotionally falling apart. Alone. Cloaked and out of sight.

On the Road to Find Out

The death of both my parents in a two-year span, coupled with the realization that I was withering on the vine, sent me on a wellness journey. I had tried many different things before I settled on these five key topics, the areas that personally saved me.

I started with a holistic, 10-day detox cleanse that provided plenty of supplements, vitamins, fiber, and healthy food. The changes were immediate (once I got over the caffeine withdrawal). Oh yes! Losing 12 pounds and 10 inches was wondrous, but detoxing my system of all the trash I'd ingested, and God knows what all was stuck to my intestine walls, changed me.

Detoxing my body cleansed me physically, mentally, and spiritually. I no longer needed blood pressure medicine. My skin was hydrated for the first time in years. I had a skip to my step. I was home-cooking again and fixing meals using real food, not the packaged garbage I'd grown to rely on.

The change and lasting impact gave me the strength and confidence to explore other areas of wellness. I was on a roll. My next conquest was TM (Transcendental Meditation), and I found peace and calmness I never knew existed. People tell me I exude a sense of harmony.

One fantastic perk that I didn't expect is that my daughter, on her own accord, followed in my footsteps as a young adult. Now, she is reaping the benefits of wellness as well, plus, it's brought us closer together as we shop for essential oils and explore spiritual retreats to voyage off to with each other.

Was my journey easy? No. I had many a hiccup along the way to the five areas I write about and feel so passionately about in this book.

Will this be easy for you? Maybe not, especially at first.

But it is so worth it! It will change you in ways you didn't know needed changing. A sense of calm and love will glow from within, and you will awake with a feeling of empowerment, knowing that you can meet the world head on.

Any change is a process, and one that we reach at different times in our lives. What worked for me might not work for you, but it may spark an interest, and one spark will lead to another. Before you know it, that spark will ignite a passion that will fuel tranquility in your life. This fuel and fortitude to challenge anxiety head on will encourage you and give you strength. You deserve this peace, calm, loving life.

CHAPTER 4
RELIEF

"Plant your own garden and decorate your own soul,
instead of waiting for someone to bring you flowers."

VERONICA SHOFFSTALL

O wn your power.

Sounds like a great place to be, in acceptance of you. But, the truth is we are all flawed, we are human after all. Instead of trying to be the be-all, end-all mom, take that pressure off yourself and relax, just a bit.

You can't fit a square peg into a round hole any easier than you can fit into a neat little box you read about in an article titled "The Perfect Mom." You are not perfect, thank goodness, we all know how dull that would be!

Here's a little secret for you. You're not broken, either, and you're not alone. We all want to feel love. We all want to feel a connection, to be at peace and heal.

What's marvelous about you is your gusto for learning, which lends itself to making lifestyle enhancements. Not improvements from a place you think is flawed but from a place that needs a little nourishment to grow, to find its strength and thrive.

Acceptance is a funny thing to understand, but the bottom line is that it's about owning your self-worth and loving yourself. Do we ever stop growing? Never. We continue our journey from a place of wholeness, and make ourselves stronger as we grow and learn new ways to adapt and change.

Whether you are a stay-at-home mom or a working mom, the challenges you face are real and painful. Suddenly you're in a situation where stress is overtaking you and impacting your ability to grow and enhance your life. Either way, you get the phone calls from school, hear the remarks during the soccer game, and pick up the pieces at the end of every day while your child has their daily meltdown – whether you work in or outside the home.

Let's face it. Some kids are just tough, and you happen to have one. While you travel this journey, often alone, don't allow yourself to go awry. You have needs, special needs that take time and nurturing. Don't overlook the stress and anxiety that often take over your day, or you may pay the price in health currency.

Throughout this book, I have sprinkled a few quizzes for you to take to estimate your level of stress in various categories, because it's important to know where you fall on the stress spectrum. You can take all of them, or a few. It's up to you.

Use the quizzes to gather information about your stress level and how it relates to the different key areas to follow in the next five chapters. Maybe you realize you need some extra support in the area of relationships, but you sleep like a rock.

That's wonderful to know about yourself; you might choose to bypass the quiz on slumber and stress.

Reflect for a moment. How much tension do you feel? Think about the last month or so, and consider a few questions for a minute:

- In the past month have you been upset about something that happened unexpectedly?
- How often have you felt that you have no control over important things in your life?
- Have you felt nervous or concerned about your ability to handle specific problems?
- Do you feel anything is going your way?
- Are you on top of things?
- How well are you coping with all the stuff you need to do?
- Are you angry when things are outside of your control?
- Do you believe things are piling up, and you're not sure how to manage everything?

If you were to give a point value to each question, where one is little to no stress and five is off the charts, you'll have a pretty good idea of how you've handled stress and anxiety this past month.

What we know about stress and anxiety today is eye-opening and discouraging, as well as encouraging. We are aware that stress can accelerate the aging process from the fascinating research done with telomeres. Stress can also cause dementia and many other illnesses over time. But you are in control of the stress and consequent anxiety and depression in your life – it does not control you. It's important to remember that as we follow our path to wellness and strength.

The areas that profoundly impacted me the most might not be the realm of your need, so these five key areas are not in any particular order. You may find that one part is especially difficult to get through or process completely, so grant yourself extra time, as this just may be the place of biggest impact for your change to occur.

Allow yourself to feel the inner workings of your biology, because certain portions may conjure up more anxiety. Be aware of how you are feeling and be kind to yourself during the process. Be gentle and reflective, and go at your pace.

Nourish

Food is life. Eating healthy is the easiest and cheapest way to combat illness, there is no doubt about this fact. We know the direct link between what we put in our mouth, and the stress we feel as an outcome of our eating habits. We also know the foods and supplements needed to combat stress.

Simple changes will make a significant impact on your attitude, cortisol levels, stress, anxiety, and depression. Bonus: adopting healthy dietary habits will change your life and change your child's behavior at the same time.

Learn how to make dietary changes that will reduce the stress in your life and restore your health. We now know there is a direct connection between your brain health and your gut, which is why this chapter comes first. It's the easiest and quickest way to see improvement in your well-being.

Peace

Find your Zen and live your life with a new calmness and in harmony. In this chapter, you will learn several simple techniques that will have a significant impact on your well-being and reduce stress and anxiety at the same time. You deserve to have guilt-free, quiet moments in your daily life. Peace generates calm – it's contagious and healthy.

Once you establish a baseline level, not only will you feel a difference, but others will notice a change in you almost immediately. Enjoy and nurture your child as you learn and teach appropriate stress-reduction methods, and celebrate the same helpful benefits together.

Love

You may need to clean your house of toxic and damaging interactions to renew your soul. Learn the difference between toxic and healthy communication and how to advocate for stress-free relationships, because you deserve them.

At the same time, celebrate the good in positive relationships, and learn ideas to nurture and sustain them. Your child will learn by example, especially if you share the benefits and comfort you realize while cleansing your universe.

Slumber

So often moms feel like sleep is a waste of time, catching a nap here or there if they get a few minutes to themselves. Sleep is of vital importance to your health, well-being, and longevity. Sleep has incredible healing powers to help reduce stress and anxiety.

Taking care of your body and mind is of utmost importance, and without 7-8 hours of uninterrupted sleep, you will suffer long-term consequences. Learn how hormone-rich substances wash your brain while you sleep, and other important healing aspects of slumber.

Healing

Learn natural healing techniques for yourself, and discover ideas and suggestions to explore and share with your child. Understand the abundance of joy this area will add to your life, and consider yourself "pampered" after you indulge in a few of these techniques. Best of all, embrace this opportunity to develop a closer bond in supportive activities while learning this art together with your child.

Give yourself this opportunity to welcome change into your life. They say half the battle is just showing up. So let's start planting the seeds for a new you. Allow yourself the opportunity to bloom and grow in areas that will spill over to others, especially your child.

You are the gardener and in order to grow, a garden needs rich fertile soil. Think of these five areas as ways to perfect your soil so new seeds can take root and flourish. Sometimes you'll need to remove weeds and debris from your soil, so your seeds can grow. That's part of the plan, part of the work.

Don't hesitate to ask questions or share your thoughts and insight as you learn to flourish.

CHAPTER 5
NOURISH

"When a flower doesn't bloom you fix the environment in which it grows, not the flower."

ALEXANDER DEN HEIJER

When I was younger and attending high school and college, I'll admit I liked the looks I use to get from strangers and friends alike. I didn't even mind the catcalls walking down the street – after all, they were strangers and had no idea what lay under my surface.

But what these flatterers didn't know at the time was that I was afraid to eat, fearful that restaurants were poisoning me with their food or that I would gain an ounce of fat and receive a stern rebuke from my father. My outer world was in upheaval with my parents' divorce and all the trauma and drama that goes along with that, but I finally had some control over my inner world.

What I didn't understand at the time was the vicious cycle I found myself in, and the healing power that the correct food can have over your mind and body.

Spending years in the deep, dark pit of an eating disorder has given me a hypersensitive awareness of the importance of proper nutrition and diet. It took me many years to get where I am today, and my journey to health was long and often lonely.

Truth be known, I loved when people commented on how thin I was. It gave me recognition and attention that I wouldn't have gotten elsewhere. Nobody, not even my family, knew that I had an eating disorder. I kept my habits very well-hidden from anyone who cared to look, and at this point in my life, no one was looking. I easily disappeared.

When I was pregnant with my babies, I effectively changed my eating habits. Once I was eating for two, I understood what I put into my mouth directly nourished a miraculous life within. I took food seriously.

But even as a new mom, I ate only enough to breastfeed my child, so I lost the pregnancy weight practically overnight. As I reflect back on these incredibly unhealthy years of under-eating, I understand now that focusing on food was a way for me to shut down my feelings and disengage from my life. Even though controlling my food intake gave me a sense of power and discipline, I was running a household virtually alone; my husband worked long and late hours. I had little guidance and nourishment.

My food battle continued for years. I often skipped meals. Instead of sitting down and eating a meal with my kids, I just ate the leftovers from my children's plates while I cleaned up the kitchen. I prepared decent meals for my children and even participated in "Pizza Tuesday Night" with other moms whose husbands worked late as well.

As I look back, I understand that limiting my food intake was tied to my desire to maintain a sense of control, not necessarily of my weight, but from my emotions as well. I was raising three children, married to a man who worked over fourteen hours a day, and my closest relative was 1000 miles away. Adding a challenging child to the mix took a toll on my health over time. Stress and anxiety became a familiar foe.

Food is our life's blood; what you put inside you fuels your engine. It's the least expensive healthcare available today. We all have the ability to take back our kitchens and infuse our lives with wellness. You need to become the commander-in-chief of your nutrition because no one else but a wise, savvy, gifted, and tenacious mother like you can make the changes necessary for you and your family.

My wellness journey started with a 10-day detox program that every member of my family participated in to one degree or another. I followed Dr. Mark Hyman's 10-Day Detox program, which I highly recommend. What can you do in 10 days? A lot. Dr. Hyman's program teaches you how to reset your metabolism, break your cravings, and lose weight. You learn interesting nutritional facts too. Did you know there is more sugar in yogurt than in a can of soda? Yes, not all calories are the same. Some of our favorite foods are highly addictive and cause major inflammation that makes us unhealthy.

What makes you sick can make you fat, and what makes you fat can make you sick. What can you do about this? You reboot. That's what this detox does for you.

The beauty of this life-changing program is that most of my family didn't even realize they were participating! My detox started a foodie revolution in my family that resulted in many benefits like reversing my high blood pressure, stabilizing my husband's type 2 diabetes, and a significant reduction in ADHD medication for my daughter. Yes, you read that correctly: a 5 mg reduction in Adderall!

Stress and Anxiety Change the Way You Eat

Everyone who's human has had an embarrassing bathroom incident. Mine happened as I unknowingly strolled through an exclusive restaurant with two feet of toilet paper stuck to my shoe. As people gazed my way, I felt good thinking they were admiring my outfit or something positive. Once I reached the table, I was appalled and horrified to find out why all eyes were on me. Did I mention I was embarrassed? I immediately grabbed the basket of bread and started to devour it until it was gone. I ate every last crumb.

There is a direct link between the stress in your life and the eating habits you adopt. Think about it. When you are in a stressful situation, two hormones are released into your body: adrenaline and cortisol. Both of these hormones are typical and healthy in a stressful situation, and they prepare you to deal with what's handed to you at the time. Sometimes adrenaline and cortisol will save our lives, but way too often, the stress is chronic and non-stop.

When you have a difficult time dealing with stress – like when your child has a meltdown at the grocery store for not getting the free cookie, for example – your cortisol levels will remain elevated throughout the day. One situation after another compounds the problem, and the impact on your body will be messy.

Cortisol is referred to as the "stress hormone" and unfortunately is the culprit for that ridiculous abdominal fat that so many of us carry around. Too much cortisol over time causes all sorts of havoc in our brain, and the result is that our brain signals go haywire by sending too many messages.

Chronic stress is too much for your body to handle. All the excess cortisol goes right to your gut, depositing fat next to your liver. A vicious cycle occurs fed by stress: cortisol is released and attempts to deliver calories to your liver at a time your body doesn't have excess calories, so your brain yells, "I need more food to fuel this body!" So, it's only natural that you give in to your brain's wishes and indulge in the richest, savory, calorie-laden food known to humanity and satisfy your body's yearning. Your brain is happy for a little while – until you hear your child crying, or you slam on the brakes to avoid getting hit by some numbskull that just ran a red light.

Chronic stress throws you into this cycle of non-stop cortisol-releasing mode. You're a cortisol-making machine! A vicious circle of continual cravings and overeating develops. Chronic stress equals overactive cortisol production, which leads to overeating the wrong foods to manage cortisol levels. This equation = major health concerns, which over time can change your adrenal glands.

Stress and eating go hand in hand. Stress will add inches to your waistline and hammer your immune system. If you get frequent colds and stomach bugs, you just might be neglecting your health.

The following quiz will help you determine if you are a stress eater and someone who will take the shortest route to the fridge when under strain. Answer honestly; this information is valuable on your quest to eliminate stressors in your life.

Use the following 1- 5-point scale for your answers:

1—No, I don't agree at all

2—I agree a little bit

3—I somewhat agree

4—Agree

5—I strongly agree

1. I find myself thinking about food even when I'm not hungry.

2. I get more pleasure from eating than I do from almost anything else.

3. If I see or smell food I like, I get a strong urge to have some.

4. When I'm around a yummy food I love, it's hard to stop myself from tasting it.

5. It's scary to think of the power that food has over me.

6. When I know a delicious food is around, I can't help myself from having some.

7. I love the taste of certain foods so much that I can't avoid eating them, even if they're bad for me.

8. When I eat yummy foods, I focus a lot on how good they taste.

9.   Sometimes, when I'm doing ordinary activities, I get an urge to eat "out of the blue".

10. I think I enjoy eating a lot more than most other people.

Calculating your score:

Add up your scores for the ten items. Scores will range from 10 to 50. The higher your score, the more likely you are to reach for the goodies and are a stress eater.

Planting a Seed ... It's easy to get discouraged after taking this screening tool. The odds are that when you live a stressful life you often feel overwhelmed, and your first action is to feed your feelings. Please know that you are starting a new journey of awareness and growth. Sit back and know that you're expanding your knowledge, learning your biology, and understanding how food affects your stress and anxiety.

Eat to Manage Stress

Are you sick and tired of being sick and tired? Stress tramples our system and spits it out in the form of fatigue and illness. There is a cure to feeling overwhelmed and anxious, and it's relatively easy with minimal investment.

The food we eat will heal the stress/cortisol cycle that you find yourself caught up in. But a change in any form isn't always easy, especially when you're making a significant lifestyle habit change that will affect you and your family.

You are not going on a diet; you are returning to healthy eating choices, most likely the eating habits your grandma recommends.

Eating whole pure foods you prepare yourself, not the packaged convenience foods that run amok in the grocery stores – what a novel idea! Add specific supplements to your diet, and you have a combination that will combat cortisol, stress levels, and belly fat. Voilá – a perfect menu for health and healing!

I know, you live a busy life and have little time at the end of the day to prepare an elaborate meal, let alone an uncomplicated one. I spent years trying different foods, but honestly, the research wasn't available then like it is today.

There is overwhelming evidence that the food we eat can and will change our health. After I revamped my eating choices, I became a health coach because I wanted to have a positive impact on the health of my family – and the changes have been remarkable. The changes are not a "diet," they are a lifestyle shift, and implementing even a few will better your life.

Cool the Caffeine

If your goal number one is to reduce harmful foods from your diet, reducing caffeine is key. When you drink caffeine, neurons are triggered in your brain, and you start to produce the "flight or fight" response almost immediately. Now, this may be a perfect response if you need to be the first through the door at a Black Friday sale, but not so perfect when you're fixing breakfast for your sweeties.

When the adrenaline wears off, guess what? You are now anxious, moody, and on the road to feeling frazzled. Next stop? You are correct – off to get more caffeine to get the same boost you got from your last cup.

The obnoxious thing about caffeine is that regular caffeine drinkers need more and more over time to get the same adrenaline hike. Continually increasing the dose results in elevated cortisol levels, and the cycle continues between your brain, belly fat, and stress. The good news is that this can be recalibrated by reducing your caffeine intake to two cups of coffee a day. After all, research does show some benefits to coffee consumption; so don't feel the need to eliminate it altogether.

Are you an obsessive drinker of joe? You better start slow to change your habit. If you try to reduce caffeine overnight, I can guarantee headaches, anxiety, exhaustion, crankiness, and often insomnia.

Wean yourself off caffeine over a week or two for pain-free results. If needed, supplement with green or white tea to ease the side effects. You will still get some caffeine but also surprisingly hefty antioxidant benefits! Try raw chocolate, it only has trace amounts of caffeine and tastes great in warm almond milk.

Planting a Seed ...Coffee Impacts Your Boobs! Women who have a history of breast cysts or osteoporosis in their families might want to stay away from a cuppa joe and caffeinated drinks. More than three cups of coffee a day may decrease bone density, which naturally increases your risk for osteoporosis, and some women report that breast pain symptoms improve when they go off caffeine or reduce the amount of caffeine in their diets. If this is the case for you, you may want to consider reducing your coffee consumption.

Split Up with Sugar!

A few years ago, I was a screaming fan of sugar. Not just any decadent dessert would do. In fact, I could pass up freshly baked cookies or a chocolate pastry in a heartbeat. But what I couldn't pass up every single solitary day was a bag of chocolate-covered peanuts followed by a package of sweet, gritty graham crackers. Yummy. Now, I understand the consequence of sugar overload, and over time, I've reduced its addictive hold on me. Was it easy? No.

Sugar is tricky. It's in just about everything we eat. It's readily available and highly addictive. According to Dr. Ron Fessenden M.D., M.P.H., the average American consumes about 150 pounds of refined sugar, plus an additional 62 pounds of high fructose corn syrup, every year. Sugar is sneaky, and it hides where you least expect it. It'll rear its ugly head in junk food and healthy food.

Does it make sense to eliminate sugar from your diet totally? Probably not. Can you decrease your sugar intake? Absolutely. But why should you care?

Interestingly, one of the greatest causes of stress is the blood sugar level in your system. Your body functions the best when your glucose level is between at 75-95 (ng/sl). The more time you spend outside that range, the more your body feels stressed.

You know that when you experience regular stress, your brain makes excess cortisol. Cortisol also manages your blood sugar levels, and if your blood sugar level changes too quickly, more cortisol will be released to regulate it. Unstable blood sugar levels will make you feel similar to being stressed out: irritable, anxious, or uneasy.

Clearly, you can't control every cause of stress in your day, but the simple action of keeping your blood sugar stable will make you more resilient. And, just like elevated levels of cortisol, unstable blood sugar will cause you to make insulin, which also causes weight gain, stress, and exhaustion.

It's extremely vital to understand that not all sugar is created equal. Once the sugar epidemic hit the media, some felt it necessary to declare all sugar off-limits. Eliminating sugar altogether is not a healthy or realistic expectation, because there is a very significant difference between natural and added sugars. Added sugars are processed and lack any nutrients. Added sugars immediately hike our blood sugar up without a single healthy benefit.

Natural sugars, the sugars found in vegetables and fresh fruit, provide many goodies, including vitamins, minerals, antioxidants and phytonutrients. The sugar in fruits and vegetables also comes loaded with fiber, which slows the absorption of sugar into your bloodstream.

It's important to make peace with sugar and find a middle ground, because total avoidance can lead to rebellion. Keeping sugar in check is about living comfortably with natural sugar and reducing added sugar.

One succulent substitute for refined sugar is pure raw honey – plus, the health benefits are marvelous. Most of the honey used today is processed honey, which means it's been heated and filtered after being collected from the hive. Raw honey is just that, pure, raw, and packed with incredible nutritional and health values.

Raw honey has many health benefits. Not only is it a natural antioxidant booster, but also raw honey promotes sleep and heals burns and ulcers. Another sweet benefit of raw honey is that eating it does not boost cortisol levels! Honey produces liver glycogen, which the brain recognizes, and because of this glycogen, the brain does not release cortisol when stressed.

Planting a Seed ... Giving up sugar cold turkey isn't easy – tough love is hard! But, if you are missing the sweetness in your diet, try sipping a hot cup of tea with a pinch of stevia, while devouring a bit of good-high quality dark chocolate or eating some sweet veggies or fruit like yams or juicy pineapple.

Hello Healthy Foods

Someone told me a long time ago that if you shop the perimeter of the grocery store, you can find all the healthy food options you need. "Don't go down an aisle for heaven's sake; you will get sucked into the junk, and before you know it your cart will be overflowing with chips and cookies and crackers." I tried shopping the perimeter once, and I ended up with meat, cheese, Starbucks, and an array of perfumed soaps and creamy lotions. Not exactly what I needed to create healthy, real-food meals.

If I had only known what foods to supplement in my diet to help reduce the disquieting feelings I had almost every minute of my waking day, I would have danced with delight and known how to shop. Well, now I do know what foods will reduce stress. It's possible to adapt your lifestyle with minimal effort and create tremendous positive change.

First, stay as far away as possible from any food that needs to be microwaved. Yes, the microwave has its dangers, but mainly avoid it because most microwavable foods come stuffed with preservatives, additives, and fillers. These chemicals will wreak havoc on your system, sap your body of natural energy, and upset your digestion cycles.

Second, remove bad fats and replace them with healthy fats. Most hydrogenated oils are dangerous for your health.

Vegetable oils such as canola, soybean, and corn oil are extremely inflammatory and will raise your cortisol levels over time, cause heart disease, stroke, diabetes, cancer, and chronic fatigue!

Healthy fats increase our hormone production, brain development, and healing, as well as reduce anti-inflammation and lower cortisol levels. There are many healthy oils to pick from, like coconut oil, olive oil, avocado, oil, ghee, and organic butter. All of these are tasty alternatives and don't alter the taste of your food – and the health benefits are unbelievable.

Third, change the meat you eat. We know from numerous studies that there are links between commercial meats and both cancer and heart disease. The grain fed to animals alters fatty acid ratios (too much omega-6 and not enough omega-3), and with added antibiotics, pesticides, and hormones, we have created a toxic mixture that overwhelms our health and leads to many disorders and chronic illness.

The selection of grass-fed and free-range meats have increased over the years, and the cost is not prohibitive as it once was, especially given the marvelous benefits. Not only are the meats free of antibiotics, pesticides, and hormones, but also they offer many fatty acids missing from the Standard American Diet like omega-3 fatty acids, linoleic acid, and arachidonic acid.

Foods that help overcome stress and reduce cortisol production are nutrient-dense, low in sugar, and have healthy fat and fiber. Shop the inner aisles of your grocery store, and load up your shopping cart with olives, avocado, nuts, seeds, beans, eggs, brown rice, sweet potatoes, turkey, and chicken.

Planting a Seed... Here are the ten best foods to eat for stress reduction. Grab your fork and dig in!

1. Green leafy vegetables like spinach are loaded with folate, which helps your body make mood-regulating neurotransmitters like serotonin and dopamine.

2. Fermented foods will keep your gut healthy. This is important because unhealthy gut flora has a terrible impact on your brain health. Have you tried fermented veggies? Not a bad addition to your diet.

3. Wild-caught Alaskan salmon is rich in omega-3 fats, which play a huge role in your emotional well-being.

4. Organic turkey breast is a wonderful source of tryptophan, which your body converts into serotonin.

5. Pistachios have been shown to dilate your arteries during stress, which means the stressful load on your heart is reduced.

6. Blueberries boost a type of white blood cell that is critical for counteracting the effects of stress. They also aid in the production of dopamine that is crucial to mood and memory.

7. One avocado will provide 20 essential nutrients that boost your health, including potassium, vitamin E and B, and folate.

8. Dark chocolate is a super antioxidant, and you don't need to feel guilty eating it anymore! You get a nice mood boost after slipping a piece in your mouth

because of the neurotransmitter anandamide that blocks feelings of pain and depression.

9. Seeds are full of magnesium, which help regulate your emotions and enhance well-being. Some excellent seeds to eat are pumpkin, sunflower, and sesame seeds.

10. Sunshine! I know, it's not technically a food, but a daily dose will stabilize your mood. Vitamin D is important for your mental health, in fact low levels of vitamin D levels are associated with an increase in panic disorders.

Say Yes to Organic (When Possible)

I planted a vegetable garden two years in a row. I was sure I had my grandpa's green thumb; his garden was huge and full of beautiful colors of the rainbow. I used to stand in awe of the ripe, juicy tomatoes and the majestic green beans, and would wait patiently for the zucchini to turn a dark green, knowing zucchini bread or pancakes would soon follow. But unfortunately, I didn't inherit his green thumb, and I now depend on farmers' markets and the organic section of the grocery store to get my fruits and veggies.

The only downside I can conceive of to organic food is that it can be more expensive than its unhealthier counterparts. Given that there are more than eighty thousand chemicals in the world today and eating even some of them impairs our health, I'm careful with my purchases. And thanks to the efforts of the Environmental Working Group, we now have a clear picture of which fruits and vegetables are most likely to be contaminated with pesticide residue.

When you can, buy organic versions of the following Dirty Dozen fruits and vegetables identified by the Environmental Working Group (EWG):

The Dirty Dozen

Apples

Celery

Sweet bell peppers

Peaches

Strawberries

Nectarines (imported)

Grapes

Spinach

Lettuce

Cucumbers

Blueberries (domestic)

Potatoes

I know that the Dirty Dozen is troubling. Just the thought that chemicals penetrate foods' skin is disturbing. But it's important information to know. You might want to consider organic when you want to eat one of these fruits or vegetables. The good news is that there is also a Clean Fifteen that the Environmental Working Group has identified as having the lowest pesticide load and the safest crops to eat!

The Clean Fifteen

Onions

Sweet corn

Pineapples

Avocado

Cabbage

Sweet peas

Asparagus

Mangoes

Eggplant

Kiwi

Cantaloupe (domestic)

Sweet potatoes

Grapefruit

Watermelon

Mushrooms

It makes total sense to cherry pick which foods to buy and which foods you might not need to buy when considering organic.

Planting a Seed ... What is organic farming, you wonder? Farmers plant crops, so the mixture of plants will keep soil nutrients in balance, or they rotate crops to make sure the nutrients stay in balance. The dirt remains in excellent condition. Organic farmers use natural means of insect control like friendly bugs, compost fertilizers, and natural compounds. They build up the soil to feed the crops and grow food that's not tainted with chemicals. Buying organic when you can is healthy for you and your family.

Sensational Supplements

Oh yes, there is a controversy over vitamins, and you've probably been recommended an assortment or a slew in your lifetime. I know I have. Over half the population takes supplements, and you can find studies that support their use and studies that claim there is no evidence to support taking them.

But one thing is clear: if you have signs or symptoms of high stress in your life, then supplements are right for you, especially if you can't get the right amount from your diet alone. Scientists have identified a few supplements that will help women who hurt from stress or anxiety. You might want to take one or two at a time and keep track of any differences. Be honest with yourself – you just may like what you see and feel.

Vitamin B Complex (especially B12 and B5 for stress relief)

Vitamin C

Vitamin D3

Zinc

Fish Oil (Omega-3)

Magnesium

Ashwagandha, an adaptogenic herb (anti-stress agents) that has amazing results in lowering cortisol

Holy basil, an adaptogenic herb mostly found in supplement form or as tulsi tea

Taking anti-stress supplements could considerably improve your stress and anxiety level in addition to a healthy diet. Despite the story you tell yourself, take action and start to make positive changes toward a new you.

It's necessary to be honest about your relationship with food in order to stay healthy and also to take care of your family. We mothers play an influential role in our child's attitude toward food and body image. The most powerful way to teach your children about food is by example. I promise you are making positive dietary changes that will not only impact you, but your child's behavior as well.

From my personal experience, my research, and my work with other moms, I know it can be difficult to make these changes. I also know that even small dietary adjustments will make a positive impact on your family.

My client Lisa takes decent care of herself and tries to cook with real food when time allows. But it wasn't until an allergist saw her daughter because of an unrelenting rash that Lisa realized the impact sugar was having on her daughter's life. Lisa tackled eliminating sugar alongside her daughter, and the changes have been remarkable for both.

Lisa states that her daughter "no longer has a rash and is calmer, she and can carry on a conversation without pausing all the time. I swear it took her forever to get a thought out because of poor word recall. Plus, eliminating

sugar from my diet resulted in my daily headaches going away and I'm more patient with her."

Lisa

Mother of Two Children, Ages 10 and 14

The old saying, "We are what we eat," is more true with each passing day. Changing our eating habits is the least expensive form of healthcare. It's not always an easy change to make, because old habits are difficult to change. As we learn and grow, it can feel uncomfortable and thorny, and not everyone will understand the new seeds you are planting.

Many other factors come into play while we are executing lifestyle changes, including the time it takes to shop and prepare meals as well as the cost of real food. But the family time gained by eating together and sharing ideas over a meal are priceless.

Just as important is the ability to have peaceful moments of time for you and you alone. You deserve the chance to have guilt-free moments to yourself in your daily life. We moms tend to complicate things. We stress. We worry. We try to do what is right. We do all the things we should do.

Moments of peace, quiet, and solitude are necessary in order to blossom – but how do you find the time in your busy schedule? Next, we will explore how to find guilt-free minutes to steal away and learn simple techniques that can have a direct impact on your child's well-being, as well as yours.

CHAPTER 6
PEACE

"Where flowers bloom, so does hope."

LADY BIRD JOHNSON

t was something about the tone of her voice, the soft whimpering whisper that broke my heart. Yes, I'd heard this passionate plea before, but this time there was a distinct difference. This time she was torturing me with her solemn sighs.

Her sweet voice was questioning why she had no friends and wondering why she was even born. As my daughter started whimpering in the back seat, I found myself feeling furious. Mad that she had to go through this drama on what seemed like a daily basis, and enraged that I didn't know how to deal with it.

I found myself mad at her, the situation, and myself. I was sick and tired of it, and I could actual feel my blood pressure start to boil. This wasn't what I'd signed up for.

Trying days like this were becoming more my norm. I needed help, and I needed it pronto. For me, my protector was and still is meditation. Without this technique in my back pocket, I'm not sure how I would have carried on most days. My only regret about meditation is that I didn't discover it sooner. It has saved my spirit and my soul.

This chapter is dedicated to the gut-wrenching anxiety that you go through, with and for, your child. It's for when you question whether you are enough and if you can keep going down this lonely road alone.

This chapter is for moms who hide in the bathroom because you need a quiet place, a peaceful place to tear up and cry without being seen. You, who often feel alone even when you are in a crowded mall on a busy weekend.

When you can find time for yourself to reflect and nourish your soul without guilt, it's a blessing you will never regret. As with so many things in life, we put ourselves on the lowest rung of the ladder. We place so many people above us, like our children, our parents, our spouse, our friends – sometimes, even strangers.

These simple self-care practices nourish your mind and your body, and add a bonus of joy and calm to your day. Adopting these practices will reduce stress and increase inner peace so you can live your life happy and healthy. Sounds miraculous, doesn't it?

Where to Begin

What does mindful mean? It seems to be the buzzword these days, so let's do some digging. Mindfulness is an ancient practice dating back as far as 1500 BCE in Hinduism, and meditation has been in existence for centuries. We have the Fab Four, aka the Beatles, to thank for introducing us to Maharishi Mahesh Yogi back in the 1960s when Transcendental Meditation re-emerged in our country again, a time when we all got by with a little help from our friends.

There are differences between the two practices. Meditation is an intentional setting aside of time to practice a specific technique you've learned. There are many ways to meditate, and it's important to find the method that fits you best.

Mindfulness is broader, because it's a way to look at the world with awareness and focus. You can be mindful at any given moment of the day, all day long, whenever you want, that's the beauty of it.

Many people think there is religion attached to meditation; I use to believe this too, but it's completely non-sectarian. I used to think I couldn't even meditate at all, mainly because I have bad knees and can't sit in the lotus position. The good news is that you can meditate anywhere (sitting in the car, up against the wall, even lying down), wherever you are most comfortable. And, you can be mindful all day long, whenever you decide.

Maybe you're feeling too stressed or feel there isn't enough time in the day to practice mindfulness, let alone find the time to meditate. Maybe it's a little scary to think about spending time with your thoughts. Maybe it's just easier to hide.

When I first started to practice meditation, I didn't know what to expect. I was fearful that I wouldn't wake up or it would change me so drastically that my husband wouldn't understand who I was becoming.

I believed all the silly myths I read in magazines, like you can't meditate because you don't have enough time, or because you can't sit still. There are lots of interesting roadblocks we place in front of ourselves to sabotage our journey. But there came a time when I chose to pursue what finding peacefulness had to offer.

Ask yourself and answer honestly: are you fulfilled, content, and at ease? The deep-down honest answer tucked away in your soul may sound like this:

"My life balance is off, and I don't know how to recalibrate."

"I feel guilty that I don't do enough for my children, even though truthfully, I don't do anything for myself."

"When I'm with my kids, I often multitask at the same time, and I don't pay that much attention or engage with them. It's hard to juggle everything at once."

"Truthfully, I'm unhappy with my kids, and myself, and I feel terrible even thinking this out loud."

Let's take a deep breath and take a quick quiz to see where your starting position is on the road to mindfulness.

Minding Your Mindfulness

Use the following 1- to 5-point scale for your answers:

1—No, I don't agree at all

2—I agree a little bit

3—I somewhat agree

4—Agree

5—I strongly agree

1. It's easy for me to concentrate on what I'm doing.

2. I'm grounded in the here and now.

3. I can tolerate emotional pain.

4. I can accept things I cannot change.

5. I can describe how I feel at the moment in significant detail.

6. I am very focused.

7. I rarely think about the past, I focus on the present and future.

8. It's easy for me to keep track of my thoughts and feelings.

9. I try to notice my thoughts without judging them.

10. I'm able to accept the thoughts and feelings I have.

11. I am able to pay close attention to one thing for a long period of time.

Calculating your score:

Add up your answers. Scores range from 11-55 points. The higher your score, the greater your mindfulness of thoughts and feelings.

Planting a Seed ... Mindfulness is starting to grab hold in the school systems. Quieting the mind brings big benefits not only for adults, but for children, as well. Practicing mindfulness improves a child's concentration, lowers stress levels, helps sleeping, and reduces disruptive and bullying behavior.

A Couple of Crazy Facts

It's pretty amazing to think that mindfulness and meditation are so easy to do and have so many unbelievable health benefits. In fact, a growing body of research suggests you can't afford not to meditate, given the stressful life we all live. Research has shown that meditation will increase attention and optimism while decreasing anxiety, stress, and depression.

One interesting study by Britta Holzel showed amazing results. Holzel and her colleagues used magnetic resonance imaging (MRI) of the brain, and scanned participants who had meditated daily for eight weeks. All the participants displayed an increase in gray matter in the brain (self-awareness, compassion, learning, memory, and introspection) and a decrease in the size of the amygdala (the area responsible for anxiety and stress). The study concluded that we could actually alter our brains, which will allow us to live with less anxiety and stress while thinking more clearly. Imagine that – we can actually alter our own brains!

And if that's not enough to convince you, here's another fact to knock your socks off. We know that there is a rising rate of heart disease among women. Coronary Heart Disease is the most common type of heart disease and the number one cause of death of women in the US. Abraham Bornstein, a Fellow of the New York Academy of Medicine, found that "Transcendental Meditation (TM) is associated with statistical significant decreased hypertension and atherosclerosis, clinical improvements in patients with established heart disease, decreased hospitalization rates and improvements in other risk factors including reduced stress and even decreased smoking and cholesterol. These findings cannot be generalized to all meditation and stress reduction techniques." There are hundreds of published scientific studies that come to the same bottom-line conclusion. TM is good for your body and soul.

One way to think of meditation is that it's similar to PE for your brain. When we meditate, we are creating strength and increasing the size of the skillful parts of our brain. A major gift of meditation is that you don't need a ton of time to gain significant benefits. I promise you that the change in your patience level, empathy skills, and degree of calm will radiate from you and affect those around you – especially your child.

How Do I Start?

You're frazzled. That's not unusual given your hectic pace, constant demands, and thoughts bombarding your mind. Sure, you may think this is right up your alley, but who has the time even to try it – let alone establish a routine?

Honestly, I didn't think I'd have the time to fit it into my day either. The funny thing about meditation is that it's addicting, at least for me. If a day does go by when for some reason I didn't find the time, I miss it terribly.

It changes you and those around you. Your daily routine is unique, so it'll be up to you to find the right time. My time is first thing in the morning after I feed the dogs and then in the afternoon around 4 pm. Some days are better than others and that's OK, there's no judgment.

Sometimes, we want to hurry the process along, but as with all good things, patience is the key to blooming. Given that there are dozens of ways to meditate, how do you get started on this road to mindful recovery? How do you learn to focus on your breath, so you're present in the moment but acknowledging your thoughts as they occur?

Mindfulness is a simple meditation type that is practiced throughout your day, but especially called up during stressful times. Let's start with a beginning meditation now.

Ready to Blossom?

Start by finding a tranquil space and a place you feel at peace. Also, consider a time of day that will work best for you. I mentioned that I meditate first thing in the morning right after I feed the dogs and the house is still calm. Sitting in a comfortable chair, on the floor, or even back in bed, find a comfy spot that works best for you. It really doesn't matter where you are.

Once you feel relaxed, check in with how you are feeling and think a bit about your intentions for the day. Are you anxious this morning? Tired? What is important to you today to focus on? Maybe you want to stop yelling at the kids so often, or feel some relief from other stressors interfering with your day. Whatever you're feeling, make it your intention for your meditation. Check in on where you're starting out mentally, physically, and emotionally.

Start to exercise your mind. I have a personal mantra that I repeat silently over and over in my mind while I calm and focus my attention. For this purpose, close your eyes and calm your thoughts. Breathe in and out, and let the stress out naturally with each breath. Try counting "one" as you breathe in and "two" as you breathe out.

Your mind will naturally wander and be bombarded with thoughts, the thoughts that will continually creep in. That's OK. Welcome the thoughts, but return to your counting mantra when you can and anchor your attention. Breathe in and out. This cycle will continue throughout your meditation, but be patient with yourself as you start to develop inward compassion. Lovingly think of your thoughts and feelings with kindness.

Thoughts are a part of you; thoughts are actually stress being released from your nervous system and are your friend. Welcome the thoughts, but always return to your counting.

Begin meditating for two minutes each morning, that's doable, right? After a week, increase by another two minutes. That's perfect. If all goes well, you'll be meditating for 10-20 minutes a day before you even know it.

You will be amazed at your levels of calmness, patience, confidence, and trust. As you journey toward a mindful life, remember that it's a daily practice. Make it a habit. Make it part of your routine. If you practice every single day, your life will change. It will transform. It will bloom.

Planting a Seed … Did you know that crying is an exceptional form of stress reduction? Humans are the only mammals who shed tears of emotion, and it's our natural way of shedding stress hormones. Crying is a natural, healthy way to relieve stress, so never feel bad about it. Shed a tear and release your stress!

Peaceful Thoughts for Your Child

There are a lot of self-soothing activities you can do with your child. All of these calm anxiety and stress, which is a win-win situation. You can teach your child how to meditate, demonstrate deep breathing, listen to meditation apps together, play, listen to music together, and take hikes in nature.

Interacting with animals is a major stress reliever, as well as laughter. Your goal is to change your child's perspective and teach her tools she can use herself throughout the day.

Different strategies will work for different children. Explore and try a few, because your child is unique, with their very own anxiety and stress. Teach your child that it's OK to let go of the stress and anxiety they are feeling, that we want to say "cheerio" to these feelings and doing these activities together will help allow the stress and anxiety to float away.

My good friend and client Alex mentioned that when she feels upset with her teenage son, she tends to see all the negative aspects of herself. Alex remarked, "I use to imagine that I'm looking at myself from across the room and thinking how can I help this crazy woman?" Now, Alex understands she can take a few minutes right then and there and quietly meditate and feel better. Alex mentioned that, "Meditation has taught me to forgive myself." What a powerful statement!

Alex
Mother of Three Children, Ages 22, 18, 16

Mary is new to practicing mindfulness but mentioned to me that "sometimes I just imagine the stress is floating out of my body like a balloon full of air. I swear it helps to lighten my load." How beautiful is this picture? Imagery has a positive

effect when working on releasing stress and anxiety and is
an enjoyable tool to use while practicing mindfulness.

Mary
Mother of One Child, Age 4

Meditation might not be for everyone, but before you make a decision one way or another, realize that the benefits go far beyond stress relief. Did you know that this technique improves attention and planning, reduces anxiety and depression, and protects the brain from cognitive decline? Meditation and mindfulness are pretty darn powerful practices, and offer an enormous return on a small investment of time.

What Gratitude Can Do for You

Do you remember growing up and listening to your parents say things like, "Count your blessings," "Say 'thank you,' honey," or "Consider yourself lucky"?

How many times have you heard these sayings? You've probably heard them at least a hundred times over the years. And you were most likely told it was necessary to practice these polite manners in order to become a decent human.

Well, guess what? It turns out your parents were right; this sage advice makes our bodies and brains healthier. Robert Emmons, a professor of psychology at the University of California, Davis and a pioneer of gratitude research, shares: "There is a magnetic appeal to gratitude. It speaks to a need that's deeply entrenched."

We give thanks to be thanked. When we feel appreciated, we feel compelled to give back. It's reciprocal, and it's what allows societies to survive, grow, and prosper.

You are so busy and harried nowadays that it's easy to forget this simple practice. Then suddenly you find yourself disconnected from others and feeling lonely, angry, or even ill.

"Gratitude serves as a corrective," says Emmons. So how can we effectively establish a gratitude ritual? You might make your morning meditation a time of reflection on what you're thankful for, or keep a gratitude journal where you write your blessings daily. It's the concerted effort to notice the wonders around us that change us for the better. Here's how.

You'll Get Healthier

Grateful people experience health benefits ranging from a reduction in mental health diagnoses to improved kidney function. It's no surprise that when you practice gratitude daily, you also tend to exercise more and are more likely to take care of yourself, including scheduling regular doctor check-ups. Did you know that writing in your journal for 15 minutes before bed will allow you to sleep better and longer?

You'll Boost Your Energy

Grateful people report that they have more strength and an increase in vitality. Studies have documented that people who wrote down things for which they were thankful demonstrated higher levels of stamina.

You'll Feel Happier

Doors will begin to open to more relationships. Studies show that people who write down one thing for which they are grateful for every day report being happier than ever before. Writing a letter of gratitude to someone who left an impact on your life can decrease symptoms of depression. Studies also show that people who practice gratitude experience more sensitivity and empathy toward others, higher self-esteem, and a reduction of toxic emotions ranging from envy and resentment to frustration and regret.

Blooming

There are many forms of meditation and mindfulness. It's important to find what fits you. Daily check-ins with your self is a stress-free way to continue to nourish your body and soul. Mindfulness and meditation practice takes on a different level of consciousness and commitment and you will know when you are ready for the transformation.

One goal of meditation is to help create a healthy gratifying life. Achieving a life of gratification is often more involved than incorporating mindfulness or meditation into your lifestyle. It's also a time when we acknowledge the goodness we've received and the grace acquired when giving back. When you take care of yourself, you have more to share of yourself. The overflow is yours to give, and love is in abundance.

CHAPTER 7
LOVE

"And the day came when the risk to remain tight in a bud was more painful than the risk it took to blossom."

ANAÏS NIN

My husband and I married on a cold, dreary December day. We were high school sweethearts and dated for eight years before we finally tied the knot. We obviously knew each other inside out, and shortly after making our commitment to each other, we moved across the country to go to graduate school, fell in love with Colorado, and never returned. We decided to make our new home together away from family influences, hoping to create our own little tribe.

Over the 30-plus years we have spent together; there have been many ups and downs, just like any marriage experiences over time. The ups include the birth of our three children, the fun we've shared, and the deep love, friendship, and esteem we have for each other. I would be remiss not to mention the downs, because every marriage has them, and about half make it through given the current divorce rate. There are the irritating trivial things that pile up over time and many disputes such as work schedules, family struggles, and inconsistencies in how to raise our children.

Raising children doesn't come with an owner's manual – and raising a spirited child is an entirely different book altogether. For me, the most difficult times in my marriage occurred when my husband and I had disagreements on how to raise our children, especially our daughter.

When you have a spirited child, the least little thing can be an opportunity for disaster. We had many differences of opinion about having clear rules, consequences, and order. It took countless discussions and learning from each other for each of us to come to terms with what would work best with our different parenting styles.

Admittedly, there was many a day I put my children first and foremost in my life, above my relationship with my husband. I was always with my kids, being a stay-at-home mom when they were school age. Truthfully, half the time my husband wasn't home much during the week, working long hours and coming back when we were all asleep.

Communication often suffered. I expected him to understand how I was feeling by osmosis, and I didn't want to take the time to explain myself. If he truly loved me, he would know how I was feeling, right? He should be aware how hard being a stay-at-home mom is, living 1000 miles from the closest relative, raising the children on my own, above all raising a precarious child. Plus, why did he think things were so perfect when I was broken, incomplete, and usually felt inferior to him?

Love and marriage almost always begin with a dream, often ones of fairy tales and greeting cards. Through the years many passages occur including the birth of children, graduations, and possibly grandchildren. Relationships may come and go, and I know this sounds cliché, but family ties do bind us together. But our immediate family isn't the only way we gain emotional care from others.

A strong network of support can be found in many other areas of your life. Possibly you have a sister or two that are close to you, or maybe you have that one good friend from college that you are in constant contact with. Often, moms find emotional support at their place of worship, where a common good connects people together.

The degree to which you have some support in your life, whether it's perceived correctly or not, means that your brain is slammed with fewer stress hormones. Let me state this a different way, because it's important to understand the consequences of this knowledge. *How you interpret the world and your emotional support directly influences your perceptions of threat, anxiety, and fear.* If you feel supported (whether you are or not), there will be less cortisol in your system, and therefore fewer feelings of stress!

Socially isolated moms will have more cortisol racing through their bloodstreams for longer periods of time. It's true, we are social animals, and connections of any kind are critically important to our health and well-being.

Let's take a short quiz together and see what your support system looks like. Is it reasonably positive or does something need work?

Social Support Systems

Use the following 1- to 5-point scale for your answers:

1—Never

2—Rarely

3—Sometimes

4—Frequently

5—Always

1. Do you have friends and family members with whom you feel at ease? Can you call on them for help?

2. When you're with your family and friends, how often do you feel you don't fit?

3. How often do you wish you knew more people you could talk to about private matters?

4. Do you feel that you did more for others in the last year than others did for you?

5. How often do you choose to mingle with your family and friends?

6. How often does your spouse/partner make you feel adored and loved?

7. How often is your spouse/partner willing to listen to you when you need to chat about your concerns?

8. How often is your spouse/partner critical of what you do?

9. How often do you feel pleased with your marriage/partnership?

Calculating your score:

Add up the scores for your answers to all the questions. Scores will range from 9 to 45. The higher your score, the more positive you feel about your social support system.

How Is Your Marriage?

The state of your marriage has a lot to do with the state of your child's behavior as well. We know that when a child is struggling or having difficulties with daily life that it may be helpful to look at the parents. Typically, one or both are having problems as well.

Often, the parents will tell others that the problem they have is directly related to their child when in fact it's the child reacting to the mother or father's stress, anxiety, and depression.

Children are paying attention. Over time they will internalize their parents' feelings; when they hear you argue or yell, chances are they will make your experience their own.

Alice, a client of mine, often tells the story of how horrible her divorce was upon her ten-year-old son. Her son picked up on many non-verbal messages between her and her ex-husband. "It's as if he could read our energy long before we spoke any words," she told me. And often when non-verbal communication and spoken words don't match, a child will trust the non-verbal part.

You are role models for what your child will expect and how they will act in other relationships. Take time to reflect and revisit your values and practice active listening with your partner. Try to remember what brought you two together in the first place.

Whether you are still married or not, the impact you have jointly on your child is enormous. Remember, parenting a strong-willed child day in and day out will put a strain on the most secure relationships. Many couples go to counseling to help with the overwhelming stress that impacts a family and marriage when confronted with the added responsibilities of a spirited child.

Planting a Seed ... It helps to post household rules that explain the values of your family. For example, "We always treat each other with respect, which in this family means no yelling, no name calling, no hitting or bullying. We are here to support each other always." Write a family mission statement together and honor everyone's input. Post it for all to see and refer to it when needed. It's powerful!

Say Goodbye to Toxic Relationships

Toxic relationships are everywhere. They bind us to people who wound us, whether it's our partner, friend, or family. Growing up in a family unit, we learn to listen, trust, and absorb what is said and heard. When we are young, our survival is dependent on every detail learned from our family ties. But at some point, our lives change.

We grow up, but stay stuck in the belief that we have to hold onto these relationships and stay loyal and connected even when it hurts us to do so. This misplaced loyalty becomes toxic, especially when you give love, but it's not returned to you. Instead, you get snarky, snide remarks and thoughts that leave you feeling bullied, small, and defeated.

Healthy families, friends, and relationships are circular. You give love, and love is received. You work through the hard stuff that continually occurs. When one person changes, the other will support your growth, not snuff it out. There is no blame, manipulation, and lying. When there is, it can only happen if you allow the toxic person to be in control.

Bullying is a red flag, and you should consider distancing yourself if you find yourself in a toxic setting. Why? Because toxic people rarely change. The havoc they wreak will be explained away as someone's fault, never their own.

Try to imagine that all relationships take up space in your life. The healthy space will be open to change, and natural ebb and flow occur. But in a toxic family or relationship, the space is fixed, rigid, and inflexible. If someone tries to stretch the space, the toxic person or family member will work until space returns to what it once was, even if they fragment the one changing the space. They will try to break you.

A common occurrence is that the person trying to change will often conform and sacrifice growth out of some misguided loyalty and find herself back in the rigid space again.

Resentment

Resentment is what honestly holds us back from feeling joyful and happy. A toxic situation will create unresolved feelings of pain, shame, guilt, and anger. If we lock this away, waiting for the person to change, life passes us by. We become victims.

A healthy relationship is one that is tolerant, accepting, and loving. You deserve this, and it's your choice now to define whom you want in your life.

You Are What Matters

Maybe you need to walk away from an old friend, a brother, sister, or parent. Know this can be done with love and with the door always open for them to reenter when they can meet you on your terms, or closer to it.

Now you must set your boundaries, boundaries that are full of grace, love, and acceptance. Then leave it up to the toxic person whether they want to stand with you or not. You are no longer that young, vulnerable girl who was dependent on her parents or other adults in her life.

You can say what matters most to you. If there are toxic people in your life, the simple truth is that they have not accepted you. Let those feelings go, not for the individual who hurt you, but for you. They might not change, but you will.

It's no wonder that people with a good network of social support have less stress in their lives. Their cortisol levels are lower throughout the day, and their immune systems are stronger because of it.

The reverse is true if you are isolated or have toxic people who play a significant role in your life – plus, you're apt to have a higher risk of cardiovascular disease and arthritis. Researchers now know that the same area of the brain lights up whether you feel physical pain or emotional pain, and the same holds true if you feel physical pleasure or emotional pleasure.

After many studies, we know that people with more social support in their lives will positively change their brain, which leads to less cortisol released! Strong relationships lessen the stress in your life.

It's a Two-Way Street

Whether you give support or receive it, the stress-reducing effects are the same. How encouraging is this? It's fascinating to understand that it's a two-way street when looking at reducing your stress, anxiety, and depression. So what can you do starting today to reduce your stress and change your brain when it comes to relationships?

Volunteer

Find a cause you believe in and can support. When my kids were younger, I would volunteer in their classrooms, and as they got older, I worked on the PTA for years. The time spent was fun and a great way to stay connected with my children, their teachers, and relate to other moms my age.

Another friend of mine didn't want to spend her free time around more kids, so she volunteered at the neighborhood library. The important thing is to give back in some way. Volunteering can reverse cognitive decline and reduce cortisol levels – a definite win-win situation!

Seek Out a Go-To Person

This person might be a therapist, a member of the clergy, spiritual counselor, or friend. The best-case scenario is that you can meet with this person to talk, either in person or over the phone. We all need to speak, discuss, and share. Transformation is a messy process, and part of the process is to want more in your life, more out of relationships, and more connections. Talk it over. Talk it out. Talk together.

Go Back to School

Take a class just for fun in whatever interest you have at the moment. Have you always wanted to learn how to knit? What about that photography class you've wanted to take since high school? A class will put you in contact with others who share your interests or hobbies. It's a great place to make new friends that you might not otherwise meet.

The bottom line is to expand and enhance your social support network because it will reduce your stress level, but make sure you're not selecting something that will add to it. You don't want to set yourself up for failure. Taking this time to build your social support will increase your self-esteem, build resilience, and start you down the path of releasing your toxic influences while forming new friendships. Whether you're the one giving the support or receiving it, you'll receive abundance and rewards in the process.

> *Working with Melissa reminded me of the importance of a support system. It hit home when she shared, "If it wasn't for my friends and colleagues there is no way I could manage the day in and day out stress in my life. My husband can only "hear" so much before he shuts down."*
>
> Melissa
> Mother of Two Children, Ages 14 and 19

Loving Thoughts for Your Child

Toxic relationships run rampant in the life of your child. Current estimates state that 40% of children will be bullied sometime during their school career. Bullies are more confident than we previously thought, but lack empathy.

Being a role model is important for your child to witness. Talk about the complex relationships you experience and how you handled them. Your child needs to talk and discuss what is occurring in their life too; otherwise, the powerlessness may lead to depression and isolation. If you suspect your child is a victim of bullying or gossip, listen to them, role-play ways to react to situations, and teach your child how to be assertive. It's important to involve the school if violence, threats, or racial slurs occur and especially if there are any threats of physical harm.

Planting a Seed ... Play with your pet! Oh, that cute, furry, slobbery dog. We know that pet owners have longer lives and fewer stress hormones raging through their system. Playing with your pet (or a borrowed one) makes you feel good and gives you a different type of social interaction. Try out a dog park or a hiking trail to meet other dog lovers. Did you know that even gazing at a fish tank lowers your stress level?

Relationships are necessary, but it's important to know that not all connections are healthy. You may need to clean house of some of the toxic relationships you've been hanging onto. They are pollution to your soul.

In most cases, this won't be an easy process to follow or achieve, especially if the toxic relationship is a family member, but it is a process that will transform your life. Ridding yourself of the negative debris and replacing it with love and unity adds warmth and richness to your life

And who knows, maybe you'll be able to sleep better too. Sleep has incredible healing powers and rejuvenating benefits. Now it's time to discover the rejuvenating ridiculous powers of slumber and the unbelievable effect sleep will have on your mind and body.

CHAPTER 8
SLUMBER

"The earth laughs in flowers."

RALPH WALDO EMERSON

I f you had a free day to do whatever you wanted, what would you do? If you said sleep, that's exactly how I felt when my kids were younger, although I would never say those words out loud, because that would have made me a bad mom. I remember one Mother's Day pleading with my husband to take the kids to the zoo without me. "It'll be the best gift you can give me," I said. "Space."

Space to myself.

Space away from others.

Space to think.

I also remember the look of concern on his face when I asked for this time alone. Why didn't he understand that I needed space and some peace and quiet? Why didn't he recognize that this was the best gift I could have received?

So what did I do when he left? I took a nap. I was tired. My oldest didn't sleep through the night until he was four years old, probably because he didn't want to miss out on anything his younger brother was doing. It didn't help that my middle child was very ill when he was 14 months old, so half the time I was waking him up just to check on him. And, three short years later when my daughter came along, both my boys were sleeping on our bedroom floor, wandering in sometime during the night and setting up camp.

The result? Chronic sleep deprivation – and I brought it on myself.

During these sleepless nights, I'd find myself pacing the house, tripping over my own two feet and wondering what in the world kind of life I was leading.

I tried catching naps when my daughter napped, which were few and far between. I resented the fact that my friends' kids slept through the night and that they looked perky and fresh each and every morning at the bus stop as they were kissing their perfect children goodbye.

How many times have you told yourself, "I'll catch a nap later this afternoon" or "If I don't get some sleep, I'm going to collapse right here and now"? Why do we act like sleep is an extravagance instead of a necessity? For that matter, why do we feel judged if we can catch a nap one afternoon? Sleep experts will tell you a nap is like rebooting your system. You let go of stress and wake up fresh. You need sleep and rest to function. Period. End of story.

Sleep has a clear-cut impact on every part of your life. And yet, in our 24/7 crazy world, uninterrupted and blissful sleep is almost impossible to find.

When was the last time you slept through the night? I don't mean a night when you only woke up two or three times, but a whole night of peaceful, blissful sleep? Missed sleep or interrupted sleep increases chronic stress because your body delivers too much cortisol even during the night.

Lost sleep means you're at greater risk for a heap of ailments such as heart disease, type 2 diabetes, illness, and obesity. Once again stress is leading the charge of another endless cycle – poor sleep leads to higher stress levels, which lead to poor sleep. You get the picture.

Do you get a good night's sleep, or do you lie awake at night reviewing the previous day's events? Are you thinking about the phone call you got from your child's teacher or the discussion you had with the principal over your child arriving late for school again?

Lying awake worrying is common when you are challenged with raising your spirited child. More often than not, late night is the quiet time of your day, so instead of allowing yourself to nod off and replenish, you are still consumed with the day's events.

If you're depriving yourself in the sleep department, you're cutting your well-being short and cutting your lifespan even shorter.

Snooze on that fact for a moment.

Sleep is integral to your health. Not getting at least eight hours of uninterrupted sleep a night can be just as damaging as eating poorly every day and never exercising. According to the *Journal of Occupation and Environmental Medicine,* women that work the night shift have a 400% higher risk of getting cancer.

Your chance of getting sick triples if you get less than seven hours of sleep a night. Your sleep is precious, and you deserve this restorative time to heal and rejuvenate.

So, how are you getting through the night? Let's see how you measure up by taking this short sleep quiz.

Sleepy Siesta Quiz

Use the following 1- to 5-point scale for your answers:

1—No, I don't agree at all

2—I agree a little bit

3—I somewhat agree

4—Agree

5—I strongly agree

1. In the past two weeks I've had a lot of sleepless nights.

2. In the past two weeks I've had a lot of difficulty falling asleep.

3. In the past two weeks I've had a lot of difficulty staying asleep.

4. In the past two weeks I've woken up way too early.

5. Do you consider your sleep to interfere with your daily activities (mood, memory, concentration)?

6. Do you think others notice your sleep problems are impairing your quality of life?

7.   I'm very worried about my sleep problem.

Add up your answers. Scores range from 7- 35 points.

The higher your score, the greater your difficulty sleeping. If you feel like you are suffering from insomnia, it's best to contact your physician.

The Miracle of Sleep

While you're sleeping, your brain and body are hard at work, busy repairing you after your day's battle. But it's important to know that not all sleep is equal. When you first nod off into a light sleep, the sleep cycle starts. Then you move into some levels of deeper sleep until you reach the deepest, which is known as REM (Rapid Eye Movement), in which dreams occur.

The entire kit and caboodle takes anywhere from 90-120 minutes. On a good night, you cycle through this process four or five times.

Intriguing new research has shown that your brain washes itself during the night. Yes, you read that correctly. Your brain actually gets washed. The brain has a special rinse that gets rid of toxins that would otherwise pile up and cause problems, including a build-up of beta-amyloid plaques involved in Alzheimer's disease.

During the day, this wash system is inactive because our brains are so busy managing our day. It only turns on when you are sleeping. Without enough sleep, toxins build up in our brains, which causes emotional and cognitive problems.

Think of sleep as your brain taking out the trash that accumulated throughout your day. Just imagine: if you piled up your trash the way you allow your thoughts to collect, you'd have a mess in your garage after a month. The same thing happens in your brain.

Sleeping also cements new memories. The thought is that direct connections between brain cells are strengthened during sleep, depending on how much we used them during the day. The important stuff we keep; the trivial data gets trashed. Do you have any difficulty remembering things lately? Many functional MRI studies have shown that one night of missed sleep will disrupt the brain's ability to make memories and remember events.

Incredibly, while you're sleeping many bodily functions slow way down, your breathing and heart rate slow. Your liver goes from detoxifying when you're awake to trying to synthesize and build when you're sleeping.

Less cortisol is released; your blood pressure lowers as well as your body temperature. Another interesting thing that happens when you snooze is that you pump out growth hormones, no matter what your age. We are always growing, whether it's new muscle cells after walking the dog to healing from a cut after shaving your legs in the shower. This repair all happens when we are enjoying deep sleep.

Stop and consider: does your child get a good night's sleep? Sleep is so important for everyone in your family, and it is often really difficult for the spirited child, especially if they take a stimulant medication.

Your Body on Sleep Loss

We've all had the experience that when we sleep less, we eat more. Back in the day, one of the fun memories of pulling all-nighters in college was deciding what type of pizza we were going to eat. As the night went on, so did the consumption of candy and soda. Once I suffered through the mid- morning exam, I naively thought the hunger pains I felt was due to all the cognitive energy spent on studying! But little did I know at the time it was my hormones thrown out of whack.

Chronic short sleep not only leaves you hungrier but also raises your cortisol production, which makes you hungrier for carbs and sweets. Is it any wonder that women that work the night shift are at a greater danger for obesity and type 2 diabetes? The elevated hormones from lack of sleep contribute to hardening of the arteries and high blood pressure. Oh, and don't forget about our tummy expanding right before our eyes.

Chris, newly divorced, explained sleep deprivation this way: "My sleep was hit and miss. After working my nursing night shift, I would get out of bed and drive to the school to pick the kids up at 3 pm. I didn't trust Adam to take the bus home, so I picked him up every day. We would come home or hang out, make dinner, get homework done, and then I was out the door again at 6:15 to drive back for another 12-hour shift. By the time I put in three of these shifts back to back, I was a total mess and had little patience with Adam. It really took a toll on both my children and me. Not to mention I was feeling like I was always cutting my kids short. Lack of sleep is like torture."

Chris
Single Mother of Two, Ages 10 and 14

7 Habits That Will Bring Sweet Dreams

Guess what the number one sleep stealer is? You guessed it. Stress! Temporary, continued stress can lead to chronic sleepless nights mainly because you can't switch your racing mind off when you continually think about your child and wonder if there's more you can do, or if there is something you haven't tried yet to ease their inner struggle. At times like these, try some relaxation techniques like breathing exercises or restorative yoga. Both will calm your mind.

My favorite go-to activity when I can't sleep? I love a hot bath with Epsom salts, baking soda, and ten drops of lavender oil. It's like hitting the snooze button for the whole night, and I wake up feeling refreshed with silky smooth skin.

Many nutrients calm the mind, relax the body, and get you all ready for sweet dreams. Look for vitamins and minerals that contain taurine, 5 HTP, GABA, amino acids and L-Theanine, calcium, and magnesium. If you prefer to go the herbal route, lemon balm, chamomile, valerian root, and passionflower are all wonderful options.

Also, for some people taking melatonin is helpful because the older we get, the less melatonin we produce. For me, melatonin has been really helpful, especially when I travel.

Do you have a TV in the bedroom? Do you fall asleep with it on and wake up hours later to turn it off? I told myself that I'd set the TV on a timer so it would turn off while I was sleeping. That splendid idea woke me up the minute the TV turned off. Now, with the advent of the iPad, it's way too easy to fall sleep with the screen near and dear to your face.

Watching any screen sets up a cycle of conditioning that reinforces poor sleep. In fact, Dr. Frank Lipman claims he's had many patients over the years develop insomnia due to this type of conditioning. Bottom line? Don't watch TV or your tablet in bed; the screen light alone keeps you from falling into a deep sleep and disrupts the sleep cycle.

Have you ever stayed in bed just hoping that you will soon fall asleep? If you do this, remember that if you don't fall asleep after 30-45 minutes, chances are you won't fall asleep anytime soon. You may have missed the sleep wave, and it could take hours before another one comes your way. You need to catch the sleep wave when it's present.

How many times have you been dead tired on your feet but when you finally go to bed you're wide awake? You missed your window of opportunity, and the wave has crashed. If this happens to you, get up and do something non-stimulating. Before you know it, you will be sleepy again and have no problem falling asleep.

For some of us, just the thought of thinking about sleep keeps us awake. You worry about not being able to sleep, which causes you not to sleep. Sleep is natural, and you need to let it flow automatically. Again, try deep breathing, don't eat dinner late, and don't exercise late in the day, because all these influence our sleep/wake patterns.

It's no secret that essential oils are a natural product with various benefits including helping us sleep. Blend bergamot and lavender oils, sandalwood, frankincense, and mandarin to create a wonderful, sleep-inducing mist in your diffuser. The pleasing aspect about essential oils is that there are little to no side effects.

Finally, there are a few snacks you can eat that are known to aid in sleep. Next time you are antsy, try half a banana with a few almonds or a cracker or two smeared with almond butter. Want something warm? Chamomile, passionflower, and valerian tea are all good drink options, and will make you drowsy in no time. A small glass of warm milk with turmeric and a pinch of cinnamon can do the trick too. Consider keeping a notebook to track what works and what doesn't. Arm yourself with this knowledge in case you need to seek medical advice from your doctor.

Sleep is crucial to your health and healing. Stress robs us of sleep, and then lack of sleep creates more stress. This mixture is a recipe for disaster. Aim for a good night's sleep every night. Your health depends on it.

Planting a Seed …Try an ylang ylang bath. The name means, "flower of flowers." This essential oil has a sedative effect on the nervous system; try blending it with sweet almond oil or jojoba to ease your stress and anxiety, and you will be amazed. Just imagine laying back in a warm bath with wonderfully scented water. Goodbye stress, hello calmness.

Sleeping Thoughts for Your Child

Parents of children who have difficulty sleeping often report problems with their own sleep patterns, which can create a vicious cycle for nighttime routines. In order to keep your biological melatonin in sync, it's important to dim the lights after sunset.

It's best for your child to sleep in complete darkness, because light pollution can disrupt hormones that affect sleep. If your child is afraid of the dark, put a night light out in the hallway until they fall asleep, and be sure to turn it off once they do.

Sleep is wonderful and healing for our physical bodies and nourishes our soul. During your waking hours there are many things you can do to continue cultivating this healing newfound spirit.

Let's explore some of these natural healing techniques, so you can continue to pamper yourself the way all mothers should. Next, we will explore the subject of healing and learn some natural techniques for you and your child to share and embrace together.

CHAPTER 9
HEALING

"The flower that blooms in adversity is the rarest and most beautiful of all."

MULAN

Motherhood brings incredible joy. I remember when my first child was born I looked around the room wondering where the light was coming from until I realized it was coming from me. I basked in pure, unadulterated bliss in my newfound love and purpose. I was desperately in love and embraced the feeling of being needed and unconditionally loved by this perfect baby.

The motherhood journey has glittering highs and deep lows. Even though I loved every waking minute, I knew I had unresolved feelings that were like a canker sore eating at my soul. My goal, my purpose, was to "mother" with all my heart and to always be there for my children, something I felt I missed growing up.

I was overprotective, which included an unrealistic desire to shield my children from everything, including loneliness, pain, and heartache. My mantra was to always be there no matter what; my children came first and foremost.

When my daughter hit roadblocks and rough patches at school or with her friends, I was there to protect her from the bullying, soothe self-esteem issues, and help with the academic challenges that set her further apart from her peers. In my case, raising a spirited child with unpredictable behavior compounded the feelings of overprotection, blame, and loneliness.

I struggled with boundaries, like most mothers. In my attempt to care for my children without hesitation, I neglected to care for myself. In retrospect, I've come to understand that the only thing you are honestly in control of is yourself.

Yes, it's crazy hard to carve time out for yourself. Others always take priority over you, as if this makes you a better mom. I'm here to tell you that's not the case. Eventually, the spring runs dry and you, my friend, are the spring. By taking care of yourself physically and with a careful balance, you can be healthy for yourself and emulate this mindset for your kids. Watching you weather storms in your newfound strength will allow your child to withstand the storms heading their way. After all, isn't this what we want for our children?

To cultivate wholesome healing and reduce stress and anxiety in your life, you might need to create a bit more "me" time. Maybe one or some of these suggestions might work well for your lifestyle, but try the ones that sound interesting to you. Once you find areas that impact your being, invite your child to join you. The stress reduction that occurs is huge, so let's share the joyful benefits!

First, let's take a glance at your "stick-to-it-ness" when it comes to exercise and physical activity. Knowing a few facts about yourself will be necessary as you enter into this area because of the energy it takes, and your ability to stay with it impacts your health-inducing results for the long haul. Gather this information and identify if you have areas of concerns and possible areas to improve.

What's Your Stick-to-it Exercise Level?

Decide on a number from 1 to 10 that best describes you, one being the most difficult and ten the best.

1. I can get up early, even on weekends, to exercise.

   1 2 3 4 5 6 7 8 9 10

2. I stick to my exercise program after a very long day.

   1 2 3 4 5 6 7 8 9 10

3. I will exercise even though I feel depressed.

   1 2 3 4 5 6 7 8 9 10

4. I stick to my exercise program even during a stressful life change.

   1 2 3 4 5 6 7 8 9 10

5. I stick to my exercise program even when I have a ton of work to do.

   1 2 3 4 5 6 7 8 9 10

6. I stick to my exercise program even when I have extreme demands.

   1 2 3 4 5 6 7 8 9 10

7. I stick to my exercise program even when my social responsibilities are time-consuming.

   1 2 3 4 5 6 7 8 9 10

8. I read or study less in order to exercise more.

   1 2 3 4 5 6 7 8 9 10

Calculating your score:

Add together the eight numbers you circled above. Scores will range from 8 to 80. The higher your score, the more likely you'll stick to a regular exercise program.

Exercise

You already know that exercise does your body good, but you might be thinking that you're too busy and stressed to fit it into your week, let alone your day. But wait – listen to the good news about exercise and stress reduction before you make up your mind.

Every single type of exercise from walking to yoga will relieve stress. A little goes a long way. Any form of exercise increases your health and well-being, and you can't help but notice an increase in your self-esteem, too.

One of the many mind-blowing aspects of exercise is that it causes your adrenal glands to release less cortisol. With *less* flight-or-fight cortisol on board, you naturally feel calmer, and with regular exercise, your blood sugars stabilize. All of this adds up to less stress and less belly fat. Now, that's not a bad outcome at all!

Exercise also pumps up your endorphins, those feel-good neurotransmitters produced by your brain. A game of tennis or even a hike in the park will release endorphins in a manner typically referred to as a runner's high. No wonder people get addicted to sports.

Exercise improves your mood and self-confidence. It will relax you and reduce the symptoms often associated with depression and anxiety; some folks call it meditation in motion! Have you noticed that when you exercise you sleep better at night? Typically, anxious thoughts, our stress level, and depression disrupt our sleep. Exercise is an excellent placebo, considering the alternative.

As you know, always consult with a doctor if you haven't exercised in a while or if you have specific health concerns. Start gradually and do what you love. Beginning a program is easy; sticking with it is harder. You might want to see if a friend will join you in a work-out. You can hold each other accountable, plus it's more fun with two!

Whatever you decide to do, the first step is to change your mindset. Exercise is not just one more thing to check off your to-do list. Make it a part of your lifestyle, and your life will change for the better. Hey, your entire family might want to get on the bandwagon and enjoy it with you.

Don't forget: the point is to reduce stress in your life, not create it. I fork over some money every month to go to a club that has shiny, clean, new equipment rather than one that feels like basic training. I like working out alone while listening to podcasts on the treadmill, and it makes the time fly by. I guess I can't get over needing to multitask! I relish this alone time, because I'm in charge of it and I find it empowering.

Planting a Seed ... After a work-out, try this calming practice that will give your feet a reflexology workout. Reflexology is a healing therapy where you use pressure on several points of your foot. Place a tennis ball on the floor and put your bare foot on the ball right beneath the arch. With comfortable pressure, move the ball between your toes and heel for about two minutes before you exercise your left foot. Ahhh, feels good, doesn't it?

Yoga

Yoga is everywhere. Nowadays you can't go to the mall without seeing at least one or two yoga centers along the way. Yoga is a mind-body movement practice that made its way to the United States around the mid-1800s but didn't become widely accepted until the 1960s and 70s. It requires movement, controlled breathing, and focus. It's now one of the most commonly used alternative health practices today. The beautiful thing about yoga is that they are many different types, and there's sure to be one that fits your personality and temperament!

Yoga is considered more holistic in nature than most forms of exercise. Combining these two physical qualities creates a meditative focus and relaxation for your body and mind.

Does it seem like everyone practices yoga? Well, there's a good reason. Over 100 studies and over 40 years of research show that yoga decreases stress and anxiety. Yoga also reduces depression symptoms and chronic pain while improving flexibility, sleep quality, blood flow, and digestion. And if that's not enough to convince you, yoga also detoxes your body, increases strength and stamina, and improves body image. Yoga is unbelievable when you think about it. This single, holistic, mindful practice will change your life.

Many different types of yoga are available to explore. It's not a one-size-fits-all kind of practice. What we do know is that yoga brings to the forefront how we might be holding our stress in our bodies such as raising our shoulders, tensing our necks, clenching our jaw, or grinding our teeth, to name a few.

Studies conducted by the Institute for Behavioral Medicine Research at Ohio State University found that yoga reduces inflammatory responses (cortisol) to stressful encounters. That, in turn, diminishes the strain that stress and anxiety place on an individual. Is it no wonder yoga studios are springing up everywhere in your community.

There is a form of yoga available for everyone from beginner to advanced, and several variations worth trying with your spirited child. Given the fact that we all have to breath, why not use your inhalations and exhalations to manage challenging situations with your child? "Several studies show that rhythmic, paced breathing balances the autonomic nervous system," says Richard Brown, M.D., associate clinical professor of psychiatry at Columbia University College of Physicians and Surgeons. Controlled breathing can help your child become more attentive and more relaxed at the same time. Plus, it's so accessible that your child can do it in the car, at school, or before an event.

Planting a Seed ... Have you tried facial yoga? Just think: if yoga is excellent for your body, how good might it be to your face? There are about 52 muscles in your face, and exercising them will alleviate facial tension as well as eye and neck strain. Doing facial exercises will keep your facial muscles flexible and subtle. So next time, don't forget to work out your facial muscles and smile!

Massage Therapy

Stress is universal, but when there is little to no relief from stress, it becomes torture. When the phone rings and you're nervous to answer because it might be your child's school, or suddenly you see your child walk down the street alone in tears, you feel the buildup of stress and anxiety in your core. Massage therapy is the perfect answer to the angst of raising your challenging child.

Virtually every symptom listed by the American Psychological Association can benefit from massage. It will lower your blood pressure and heart rate, and increase endorphins, serotonin, and dopamine. Is it any wonder you feel calm and relaxed after a massage?

Researchers have shown over and over that one session of massage therapy will lower your cortisol levels, which is why massage therapy and stress relief go hand in hand. You deserve to try this at least once to feel the benefits for yourself.

Wouldn't it be wonderful if taking care of your body and soul was at the top of your priority list? The interesting fact is that if you take this step for yourself, everyone wins. You will feel, look, and be far healthier. The stress relief alone will improve your state of mind and improve your reactions to your child.

Planting a Seed ... When you experience situations that make you feel stressed, anxious, or powerless, it may conjure up memories of your childhood when you experienced loneliness or sadness. Be loving and caring for your inner child during these times. Know that you will get the two of you through this anxious time. Give yourself a mental embrace – and hug your child while you're at it!

Essential Oils

I never leave home without my essential oils, even if it's in the form of a small candle. I enjoy my destination once I get there, but I find travel itself very stressful. Traveling with kids only adds to my stress and anxiety, and it takes me a day or two to finally unwind only to leave to go home before I know it. That is why I started using essential oils. Truthfully, I use them daily, but oils are a friend in need when I travel.

Aromatherapy essential oils have been a trusted practice in cultures for over 5,000 years. Essential oils are made by using medicinal plants, herbs, roots, trees, and flowers that are grown throughout the world. Today you can find over 40 different therapeutic-grade oils in health food stores and online.

There are three distinct ways to use essential oils: via aromatherapy, through ingestion, or by applying topically. Personally, I have not ingested essential oils, so I will limit my discussion to aromatherapy and topically only, because I can personally speak to these two techniques.

Aromatherapy for stress and anxiety is popular because our sense of smell is strong, and we process a ton of information through our olfactory senses. The area of our brain that processes smell is the same area of emotional processing and memory recall. It's fascinating to think that when you inhale an oil, molecules enter your nose and create a mental response in the limbic system of your brain. These reactions regulate stress or calming responses.

Aromatherapy can be added to the bath, which delivers a fabulous spa-like experience. Of course, you can open the bottle and sniff (ahhh...) if you want. A diffuser is easily available in stores, and you mix the oils with water. Diffusers are a very popular way to dispense aromatherapy and have the added benefit of humidifying the air. I have a friend who wears oils as her perfume of choice. She swears lavender keeps her calm all day long.

When using essential oils topically, it's best to mix with a carrier oil. Applying essential oils directly to your skin can cause irritation, especially if your skin is sensitive. Fantastic carrier oils to use are coconut oil, olive oil, or grapeseed oil. When applying oils topically, you will love not only the heavenly scent but also the added moisture of using oils. Take your time massaging the oils into your skin. Savor the feel and essence of this moment.

The Top Six Essential Oils for Stress and Anxiety

Lavender Oil is by far the most popular essential oil in the world and my go-to oil. I apply it to reduce stress and anxiety, and it keeps me balanced. Lavender oil is considered a nervous system restorative and helps with stress, anxiety, panic attacks, sleep, and general nervous tension. It helps with inner peace. Lavender oil gets the gold star for an excellent essential oil that works with so many problems, and the bouquet is fantastic! It's also safe for children.

Rose Oil is my favorite smelling oil. Whenever I catch its scent, I'm immediately drawn back to memories of my mom. She loved roses and was incredibly proud that she was born and raised in the City of Roses (Portland). We had dozens of rose bushes in our yard growing up. How can I not think of her? But this is also the power of scent. The main benefit of rose oil is that it's very settling to the emotions. It's the second most popular oil after lavender and is also known to relieve stress, anxiety, and depression.

Vetiver Oil has a tranquil, soothing, and grounding energy and helps stabilize and calm trauma patients. Vetiver oil is considered a nervous system tonic, because it reduces hypersensitivity and the jitters. Vetiver oil is completely safe for kids of all ages. Studies by Dr. Terry Friedman found that the relaxing and calming properties of vetiver oil helped children combat their ADHD and ADD symptoms by using it in a diffuser at night. It's also beneficial for panic attacks and shock. It's pretty amazing that this oil can have such tremendous effects on our well-being.

Bergamot Oil has a nice citrusy scent and is especially useful for stress, anxiety, and even pain relief. You can find bergamot in Earl Grey tea. The neuroscientist community has identified that bergamot changes synaptic plasticity in the brain, which is a remarkable outcome for people under a lot of stress. Bergamot is safe, but it can increase the risk of sunburn and rash when out and about.

Chamomile Oil is thought to be one of the oldest and most versatile herbs known to man. There are numerous benefits and virtually no side effects unless you are allergic to ragweed. Chamomile antioxidants are found in the plant's oils and are one of the reasons why it has natural healing properties. Of course, there is chamomile tea made from the plant's leaves, which is a tasty soothing drink.

Chamomile is often used to calm nerves and reduce anxiety caused by stress because its scent travels right to the olfactory part of the brain. It turns off tension and decreases the body's stress response, otherwise known as cortisol. Scents are a straight road to emotion and memory and are one of the quickest ways to achieve psychological results.

Frankincense Oil is incredible for treating anxiety and stress because it creates a peaceful and calm energy. In aromatherapy, it helps deepen meditation and quiet the mind. Want a quick stress relief idea? Add a few drops of frankincense oil to your bath for instant stress relief. You can also add it to your diffuser to help combat anxiety and stress. Some people think frankincense oil can increase your intuition and spiritual kinship.

When buying oils, avoid oils that say "fragrance oil" or "perfume oil." This type of oil may be synthetic and won't give the health benefits mentioned above. Look for oils that say "pure essential oil" or "100% essential oil" for the highest quality. Finally, don't ingest oils or use directly on the skin without a carrier oil. It's critical to understand how best to use oils for your safety and best possible health benefit.

Pamper Yourself

Getting started is the hardest part of any journey, and knowing you, I understand it's hard to set aside time for yourself especially when you are so busy with your child. So I'm going to help you take that first tenuous step.

Do any one of these excuses below sound familiar to you? We've all used them in one form or another while attempting to find time for ourselves once we've taken care of our child.

"I'll start a yoga class after my kids go back to school after spring break."

"I'll stop at the health food store tomorrow morning to pick up some essential oil."

"I need a good night's sleep, and then my neck will feel better. Besides I don't have time this week for a massage."

A little confidence is what you need to make a baby step toward change. You've already made tremendous progress by reading this book. After your first step, take another step tomorrow, and before you know it, you'll be at your destination. Don't forget about yourself and if you ever think about giving up, check in with me. I'll be here for you in a heartbeat.

Remember that self-care is directly linked to self-love and self-respect. It's important to be mindful of exercise, because your health is important to not only you, but for your family as well. Physically caring for yourself tells your children that you value your health and that you want them to appreciate theirs.

Planting a Seed ... Enjoy a relaxing, stress-free bath by adding ten drops of your favorite essential oil to 1/2 cup Epsom salt. Don't forget these five tips for the perfect bath.

1. Kick everyone out of the house or at least your bedroom.

2. Log off all screen time.

3. Listen to your favorite tunes or soak in complete silence.

4. Pour yourself a tall glass of water with a slice of lemon. Sip throughout your bath.

5. Light some candles and dim the lights.

Enjoy your precious 20 minutes of alone time and relax and enjoy your stress-free slumber tonight.

I noticed one day while watching my daughter's soccer game that my friend Pat was not sitting with us on the sidelines like she usually did. I caught up with her later and asked why she wasn't hanging out with us. I thought her answer was genius. She said, "I finally wised up. Now when I go to soccer games, I bring my tennis shoes and I walk around the field the entire time. It sure beats sitting on the sideline with other moms, especially since I have a tendency to gossip."

Pat

Mother of Three Children, Ages 6, 12, and 15

After working with Brit, I asked her what her favorite part of her self-care routine was. I so resonate with her answer because I love this ritual myself. Brit shared, "There is absolutely nothing I love more than to crawl into a hot bath full of Epsom salts, baking powder, and lavender oil. Sometimes I add Vitamin E oil to the water too. It's my one indulgence at the end of a stressful day, and boy, do I sleep soundly that night!"

Brittany

Mother of Four Children, Ages 3, 8, 10, and 14

Following all or just a few of these five key areas will help make a transformation in your life and the life of your child and family. There is no doubt about this, and it's proven in many published research articles.

I understand your dilemma: it's hard to find the time, and even if you did, you feel guilty spending it on yourself.

I get it.

You have a spirited child.

I lived it.

In fact, at some point in my life, I think I loved it.

I think I liked being a martyr.

But that was the old me, and it took me years to accept the clarity I have today.

What about your child? How can you make these substantial changes in your life and not feel like you're shortchanging your child, your husband, or your entire family? And we aren't talking about minor changes. We are considering magical changes that will affect everyone in your universe, if you allow it.

What is obstructing your forward motion from trying one step, let alone two or all five?

Guilt?

Anxiety?

Stress?

Would it help to make this transition into a whole new healthy being if you were able to bring your child along for the journey?

Well, I've got you covered with this next chapter, Taking Root.

No more guilt or anxiety over taking a step back and reflecting on yourself and your needs.

No more sleepless nights wondering if the action you take might positively influence the others around you.

This chapter is for you and your child, my friend. I hope and pray it allows you the opportunity and strength to share your self-care journey together.

CHAPTER 10
TAKING ROOT

"A flower cannot blossom without sunshine, and man cannot live without love."

MAX MULLER

W hen I was a little girl, my mom would patiently sit with me while she taught me how to knit and purl. Inevitably, I would pull the yarn too tight, end up with a cockeyed mess, and have to rip it out and start my scarf over.

My mom had the patience of a saint. A few years later I made my first sweater in Girl Scouts and had to learn all sorts of new stitches. I know she was as proud as I was when I finally finished my light blue sweater - holes and all.

Memories create a piece of our soul that no one can steal away. Someone might say, while reminiscing about his or her childhood, that those times are long gone. "That was back in the day when there were no phones or other distractions, back when people had time."

Please say it isn't so. The time to enjoy your spirited child is now. Spirited children are more sensitive, perceptive, self-motivated and persistent compared to an average child. Enjoy creative times together and occasionally let them lead – you will be amazed at the direction your child creates to reach their magic road. Go along for the ride and savor the journey!

Not too long ago, my daughter and I made aromatherapy candles together – but not just any ordinary candles. My daughter is an avid animal lover, and she has a kooky sixth sense especially about dogs, she attracts them like bees to honey. She researched various essential oils to find the exact correct mixture that would help calm her anxious dog.

Now that my daughter is a young adult, we spend a ton of time together. You'll find us eating brunch together talking politics, arguing over the ending of *Gilmore Girls,* deciding what spiritual retreat to attend together, and forever bound by our deep passion for all things related to doodles. Watching her mix the oils and discussing their pros and cons made me extraordinarily proud of her.

Ever since high school, my daughter has used essential oils daily, either in her bath or in a diffuser. She completely revamped her diet to manage adrenal fatigue that was making her sluggish and fatigued. My daughter meditates daily and is working hard at ridding herself from her toxic lifelong friends. She's taken so many huge steps, steps that have changed the trajectory of her life. Have I mentioned how proud I am of her?

Did my daughter watch and learn? Maybe a little bit. But mostly, she knew what I was doing because every step of my way, I shared with her. Did I force her to follow my path? No, she decided on her own if and when to forge her trail that eventually led her to self-discovery and self-care.

My sweet, loving daughter will continually need my love and support, and if she stumbles along the way, I will always be here to help pick her up. My heart is full when I think of who she has become. Her journey is new and fresh with a door wide open to explore her life. What more can I ask for as her mother?

> *We were cleaning up the kitchen, after melting the soy wax for the dog candles, and I asked my daughter to share her thoughts about her earlier years. She quietly whispered to me, "The way I feel now compared to a few years ago is a complete 180-degree change. Before, I was constantly bombarded by negative thoughts throughout the day and thoughts that I believed about myself. Now, I still have some negative thoughts cross my mind but without the frequency and intensity as before. I now have more positive thoughts about everything, and it's truly a wonderful feeling! I also don't feel like I get irritated as easily and can tell there is an improvement in my memory."*
>
> My Daughter

Hopefully, you too learned about what stress and anxiety can do to your health and well-being. The ability to control your cortisol level and therefore your stress level is extraordinary. The powerful feelings of self-confidence are hard to hide, and will spread their wings out to all member of your family. And learning about this topic will certainly benefit your child as well, especially if they get to travel this journey of change with you.

Allowing your child inside your new lifestyle changes will give her the opportunity to learn about her brain, her feelings, and her entire body. What a wonderful gift! Just think, by living a life of change, you will give your child the opportunity to watch and learn from you.

She will discover how to express thoughts and feelings into new words, and she may learn the difference between suffering silently and actualizing feelings for the very first time. With your guidance, your child will understand and learn about her beliefs and practice healthy choices.

What an incredible legacy to share. But, you might be asking, "How do I start this journey with my child?" Well, there is so much to do and know, and certainly what is healthy for an adult might not be healthy for a child. You don't have to look any further than this chapter to get you started on a life-changing journey together.

It's important to accept the knowledge that the best coping strategies for your child are ones that put her in control. Listen, I get it. I wanted to control my daughter's environment a lot, mainly because I wanted to protect her. It took me a long time to realize that when I said she could skip soccer practice, or play dates, or birthday parties, it did not make her stress lessen or go away.

If I had a do-over, I would understand that she needed to learn to identify the stressful situation and come up with her plan to deal with it, with my help and guidance. It's also paramount that you understand that stress is contagious. Your child will be stressed if you are stressed. It's that simple and that complicated.

Now that you have the tools to understand your stressors, you can be a role model in her eyes as she emulates your healthy stress management and self-care.

Nourish

There are many effective ways to combat stress and anxiety in children of any age. Diet is one of the most comprehensive and significant means to eliminate stress and lower cortisol levels. For years physicians have known that a high protein low carb diet is best for stress reduction. Fat is good for behavior change too, but it must be the healthy fats.

Increasing protein alone is a dietary change that will help with energy level and concentration. Unfortunately, as we know all too well, the standard American diet is filled with sugar and simple carbohydrates, which have a detrimental effect on dopamine levels in the brain. So, here's the nitty gritty that you need to know now in order to make significant changes in your child's diet.

Steady the Blood Sugar

If you maintain blood sugar levels throughout the day, you can decrease levels of anxiety. Your child needs a good start to her day to set the stage. A typical breakfast today is filled with simple carbohydrates, I was guilty of feeding my kids frozen waffles or a bagel, assuming it was a hearty meal. Was I ever wrong! Not only was it terribly unhealthy, but also I'm sure it's why they wanted to fall asleep mid-morning!

Remember the breakfasts of yesterday? Scrambled eggs and bacon have moved to the sidelines, mainly because of the time involved in preparing such a breakfast. But the bottom line is that protein is filled with the ability to stabilize dopamine in the brain.

Maybe you could consider making breakfast with the food you typically feed for lunch, like a slice of turkey rolled up with cheese, a fruit-veggie smoothie, a handful of nuts, vegetable soup. How about gluten-free bread smeared with coconut or almond butter?

The omega-3 fats are super healthy for a fresh start in the morning, and if you include extra snacks for when your child rides the bus home at the end of the day, she will be in a better mood when she walks in the door after school. Food is brain medicine.

Ditch the Dairy and Wheat

Many children are allergic to dairy and wheat, and what's so exasperating about this is some pediatricians won't test for this allergy or the tests they order are not sensitive enough to show if there is a problem.

Your mom gut is powerful. Notice if your child is sniffling after drinking milk. Gluten intolerance can affect the skin, joints, teeth, nervous system, and even mood and behavior.

Does your child get an upset tummy or soft stools? The bottom line is that if your child is congested or itchy, it's an added stress in their body and will increase their anxiety level. Consider ditching the traditional cow milk and try coconut milk, almond, or soymilk. They are loaded with more vitamin B too, which is a mood-enhancing supplement.

High Tea?

Wouldn't it be fun to take your child to a teahouse and experience the atmosphere and aroma sifting through the air? Tea is ancient and is known to be an herbal remedy for digestive problems, calming your mind and creating other amazing effects. Many teas are caffeine-free, too, but make sure and read the labels.

Is your child restless and having difficulty falling asleep? Next time have a cup of chamomile tea together while you slowly feel slumber heading your way.

At the end of a cold wintery school day when your child comes in frazzled and hurried, sit and have a cup of passionflower, lemon balm or jasmine tea together just for the fun of it. It's a great way to catch up.

Of course, there are added benefits to this cozy time spent together besides sipping tea. Finally, wouldn't it be nice to have a warm cup of tea when you're struggling with your math homework? Tea has many health benefits for you and your child, so have fun experimenting with different tastes, and learn what teas are used for which ailments. There is a lot of thought-provoking fun to be had here!

The Bottom Line

We all want to feed our child the correct food for their growing brain, especially kids who suffer from stress and anxiety. Here are a few tools of the trade to keep in mind while making food choices and meal planning.

- Remember the importance of water. Our brains are 80% water and anything that dehydrates it, like caffeine, impacts your child's thinking and ability to make decisions, not to mention increases cortisol production.

- When deciding between food items, serve high-quality choices. High-calorie foods will drain your brain, and your child's development will suffer. One cinnamon roll can cost your child 720 calories, load their system with sugar, and hype up their cortisol production.

- There are good carbs and bad carbs, but the good news is you know the difference. Sugar is not your child's friend, and the less she ingests of it, the better. High fiber carbs are excellent for your child, so boost the fruit and veggie intake.

- Remember, fat is not your enemy. Healthy fats are critical to your child's brain health and overall development. Once all the water is removed from a brain, the solid weight is made up of 60% fat. Focus on the healthy fats that contain omega-3 fatty acids found in walnuts, chia seed, flax seed, and dark leafy vegetables. When I make breakfast smoothies, I always add these ingredients along with fruit and my kids don't even realize what was in the healthy potion they just slurped down.

- Protein is a gift. It stabilizes blood sugar, sharpens focus, and provides the nutrients for brain development. Your child needs healthy protein throughout the day. Excellent sources of protein include turkey or chicken, nuts, bean, and green veggies.

Supplements

Finally, always check with your child's doctor before adding supplements to medication. Some supplements interact with drugs, so caution is needed. That said, no matter what, give your child a multivitamin and multi-mineral supplement daily.

The old school way of thinking is that if you eat a balanced diet, you don't need vitamins, but honestly a balanced diet is a thing of the past. Protect your child today with a multivitamin and multi-mineral supplement that provides 100% of the daily allowances. There are many choices available, and most are offered in a chewable or gummy option that kids don't mind taking.

The other needed supplement to add to your child's diet is omega -3 fatty acids. It's difficult getting this needed nutrient in your child's daily diet, so there are yummy gummy options available for this too.

With my daughter's journey, I've learned many other options to help calm the brain and to supplement low amino acids in the brain. Please feel free to contact me directly to find out more about these options.

Peace

If your child's school is anything like my child's, PE has been drastically reduced. Heck, PE two times a week for 45 minutes is hardly enough for a growing child! It's outrageous, especially since the USDA and Department of Health and Human Services recommend that kids six years and older get a minimum of 60 minutes of exercise seven days a week!

Let's face it, our children are not getting this amount, and it's especially frustrating when we know that exercise increases mood-boosting brain chemistry and is crazy impactful with our spirited children.

Child Yoga

Yoga involves quieting the mind and is an excellent practice for children to adopt and learn. One of the best postures to teach your child is the Standing Mountain Pose. Why is this? The Standing Mountain Pose positions us to become centered, which is of vital importance for children who are experiencing anxiety. Try the mountain pose together! Stand up straight and tall with your feet parallel to the floor and your arms by your side, roll your shoulders back, keeping your chin parallel to the floor. Now, engage your legs by pressing the heels of both feet on the floor. Can you feel your kneecaps lifting and firing your quads? Finally, lower your gaze but not your chin, and open the palms of your hands while you breathe deeply in and out.

Another remarkable position is the Child's Pose. Guide your child down on all fours and then move her hips back until they land on her heels and her forehead is resting on the floor. Begin to rub your child spine down and start over from the top. Tell your child to visualize water running down her spine clearing out all the toxins from her body.

Both of these basic yoga poses will alleviate stress and anxiety especially if practiced every day. Yoga is tremendous for our children. Currently, many community centers offer yoga classes for children and families as well as DVDs, CD's and tapes. There are so many options; all you have to do is choose!

Letting Go

Letting go at the end of the day is a beautiful ritual to teach your child because it's their creation and no one else's. This ceremony will signify getting rid of any lingering thoughts or negative feelings hanging around at the end of the day.

Maybe there is an activity your child already does every evening, like walking the dog or riding her bike. It could be something as simple as brushing her teeth. The important thing is to let your child decide and explain to them that this activity now is done with intention.

For example, while she is washing her hands, she imagines the stress and anxiety of the day washing down the drain, or with every turn of the bicycle pedal she might be releasing an event or conversation she had earlier in the day.

Maybe your child wants to adopt a mantra to repeat during this letting go activity such as, "I choose to keep the positive thoughts and let go of the negative ones." The idea is that your child decides on the ritual and mantra.

This ceremony is hers and hers alone. Just remember it is the intention of letting go that makes this very powerful, not necessarily the words she chooses to say.

Love

School and friends are of utmost importance to your child, and if your child has high anxiety on top of everything else, this can be an especially traumatic time. For our spirited children, it's fairly common that they have problems making, keeping, and interacting with friends.

Peer pressure comes into play during this time, and the resulting insecurity can undercut all of your child's self-confidence you so diligently helped to raise all these past years. It's heartbreaking to watch your child navigate these treacherous waters when it's so easy for things to go awry.

What can you do during this stage of life? It's important that you anchor your child, be there for her, stay connected, and be a source of support. Enjoy her activities, whether it's sports, dance, martial arts, or Girl Scouts. These events can foster ready-made friendships with kids who have similar interests and talents. Hopefully, this peer group will be a source of positive influences and social interactions.

Take pride in your child and support whatever activity she decides to pursue by attending events, volunteering, or hosting gatherings for the group. Remember, it's important for your child to widen her social circle, especially if she is struggling with peers at school. Don't assume it's all her fault. Support her ability to reach out to others.

The family is the one constant in your child's life and whom she will be able to rely on and go to during times of strife and difficulty. She's lucky to have you as a mom.

Slumber

The importance of sleep is no laughing matter. Our children with increased anxiety and stress have a particularly hard time transitioning to bedtime, let alone falling and staying asleep. As you now know, one of the main reasons sleep is critical is so we can recover from the stressors of the previous day or week.

Sleep is so essential that on average, doctors recommend that children six to nine years old need ten hours of sleep, children ten through twelve need nine hours, and adolescents need eight to nine hours of sleep each night. Easier said than done, at least in my home!

Winding down at the end of the day should begin a good one to two hours before bedtime. Have your child finish all homework, computer games, and TV-watching a good hour before going to bed. Use this hour before bed as a time to read together, tell stories, or listen to music.

Indulge in a light bedtime snack and make sure to add protein and a light carbohydrate, which will encourage melatonin production. Ideal snacks are yogurt with some apricots, a slice of turkey, herbal tea, or a bit of cottage cheese – nothing too heavy, but enough to stabilize blood sugar throughout the night. And don't forget about the power of a nice warm bath before sleeping!

Research tells us that the ideal room temperature for sleep is between 60-65 degrees for children and adults. Use a night light in her room, especially if she is fearful of the dark, and don't forget about all the cozy blankets and stuffed animals that may calm your child, too. Another option to try is white noise. Adding ambient sound can help to turn off the anxious thoughts by creating an outside reference point, which will help her fall asleep.

Finally, the easiest way to reduce anxiety is to get up early in the morning. Start the adjustment slowly by 5 minutes and then 10 minutes over the course of a week or two, reaching 15-30 minutes within the month. You will find that moving up the time to rise will help her body be ready for sleep at the end of the day.

Your child is no different than you. Sleep is pivotal, and lack of sleep will increase her anxiety and ability to self-regulate throughout the day. Creating a positive sleep environment is helpful to establish this important health requirement.

Healing

If you've found that traditional therapies are not doing what you expected, it might be time to look at some other natural remedies for your child. Natural treatments have been used for centuries and in conjunction with traditional techniques healing may occur.

Massage

First and foremost, make sure the therapist is certified and has expertise in child massage therapy. The touch used is more gentle and soft and can be done in a chair or even standing. Make sure the therapist asks permission and your child agrees before the therapy begins.

The benefits are numerous, including a decrease in stress, anxiety, and heart rate. Hugs are huge, too! Touch, in particular, reduces stress and promotes the growth of myelin, the insulating material around our nerves. It's possible to give your children massages yourself using simple techniques at home. What a bonding experience for you and your child!

Acupuncture

I have a good friend who swears by the acupuncture treatments her son with autism receives weekly. This therapy, more than any other, has shown the greatest impact on his demeanor. Again, make sure your therapist is licensed and works with children. The thin needles don't hurt, but even so, the treatments can be done with your child sitting on your lap. The benefits are rich and include reducing stress, anxiety, attention deficit disorder, depression, and many more ailments.

Biofeedback

This painless, noninvasive technique is often used to treat children with anxiety and pain. Kids love this procedure because they will sit in from of a computer monitor watching games, cartoon, and stories, or listening to tunes or songs. As the images or sounds change, your child will learn how to change their physical state and feelings. It's amazingly beneficial and so exciting to watch the improvements this technique affords!

I'm hopeful the above information provided you with ideas and thoughts on how to share your newfound care with your child. A balanced and healthy protein-rich diet with less sugar and processed foods is an easy change to make and one that I bet your child won't even notice.

Getting active even if it's as simple as taking the dog for a walk after school is a proven mood booster. Ride a bike, go for a hike, enjoy a day building a snowman, these are all ways to be active together.

Helping your child understand the toxic relationships in their life and how to let them go is a tool they will use for the rest of their life. And finally, proper sleep is mandatory for a growing child. Lack of sleep or poor sleep only adds to your child's anxiety and their ability to self-regulate. Plus, it's fun and bonding to create sleep rituals together.

As I reflect on my delightful weekends with my daughter, days I never thought in my wildest dreams would be full of positive life and light, I'm grounded in the knowledge that my life changes helped her life change. It's been entirely reciprocal, because without her I wouldn't be me and without me, I'm not sure where she would be. These are words I never thought I would be able to say, but here I am, speaking our truth.

CHAPTER 11
BARRIERS

*"If we remain afraid and closed off, we never
know what it feels like to bloom."*

LORI SCHAEFER

'll never forget the time my girlfriend from college, who I
hadn't seen in years, asked me how I got the scar between
my eyes. Feeling stunned, eyes downcast, I felt the heat
rising from my neck circling and burning my entire head.
Seriously? A scar? I was embarrassed! I bet by now the "scar"
looked as deep as the Grand Canyon.

With a half-smile, I admitted it was a permanent frown
line. I was a bit shocked that she brought it up in the first place.
Heck, I hadn't seen her in years, and those were the first words
out of her mouth!

My mind got the best of me, and I started thinking ...
what if my frown line was a scar from a knife attack I survived

while walking to my car alone late at night all by myself? My imagination ran wild as I quickly tried to think of a story I could share about why I have a "scar" between my eyes. I immediately tried to think of a crazy-exciting badge of honor story that would make her feel jealous or in awe of my exciting and thrilling life. Imagine her surprise when I 'fessed up' that it was a frown line, due to my constant negative mood.

A simple frown line is what created my deep "scar," like a flashing blinking light screaming all my misery out to the world. I was humiliated having to admit this to my lifelong friend, but truthfully, even more ashamed to admit it to myself. Was I that unhappy that I ended up with a badge of defeat front and center between my eyes? Yes. I was.

It wasn't that long ago that I started making positive changes for myself. I think of it as planting a garden. Along the way, I cultivated and planted new seeds that blossomed into my life-changing habits. At the same time, I allowed myself to stop feeding old ways that eventually died from lack of nourishment, and I continue to this day to weed them out when they rear their ugly heads. Obstacles or barriers are a part of our life, and it's how we choose to meet them that determine the changes we will make.

I can honestly say that my health has never been better. I went from chronic headaches, sleepless nights, and a miserable demeanor to a headache-free, peaceful slumber and feelings of tranquility almost immediately after making the changes I identified for myself.

We all face hurdles, especially when trying to change habits about ourselves that are ingrained in us, sometimes from birth. It wasn't easy for me to justify the time I needed to devote to myself to achieve my harmony. This meant time taken away from my children, and it didn't feel like it was in my DNA to contemplate making a change this drastic. But with each little mental budge, I quickly understood the impact this crowded space was having on my psyche.

Coming from the world of "should," this was no easy task to challenge, let alone change. It took many nights of coaching myself away from familiar inner thoughts such as, "I should be cleaning the house right now instead of meditating." "I should be watching my son practice soccer instead of shopping for fresh fruit." "I should be volunteering at my daughter's school instead of going to Pilates."

Wiping away the negative impact of living with "should" was one of the greatest gifts I gave myself. The permission to sometimes put me first without guilt, knowing that this act made me a better person, mom, daughter and wife. I learned a wondrous, lifelong lesson, which took time and energy to accomplish, and I know that with support, you can too.

If you're reading this book and have gotten this far, chances are you're considering making some of these steps permanent changes to your lifestyle. Congratulations! The first rung is the hardest to reach. And with each new step along the way, your child will be there with you. Your personal changes will impact your child, and your growth and happiness will be contagious and create a whole new energy for your family.

One thing you might want to do is share with your partner or a friend the changes you plan to make in your life, because these will not only have a tremendous impact on your well-being but will also positively impact your family, as well. Explain the health benefits gained by eating correctly, practicing mindfulness, establishing wholesome habits, and changing or eliminating screen time from your nightly routine.

If you currently take medication for high blood pressure or cholesterol, share from the rooftop the impact these changes have on your health and happiness, especially when you lower or eliminate medication altogether. Having the support of your family and sharing the excitement with them will stimulate changes for all.

My hope is that you are now armed with real-life knowledge to implement change or at least consider it, not a bunch of theories that you will soon forget. Remember that you do not have to do this work alone, and understand that it's a sign of strength to ask for help.

Imagine the world where you make these changes, and your child and family learn by example and follow your great steps. There is no greater gift that you can deliver to your family or yourself than self-care. Your commitment to enhancing your life will create a healthy body, mind, and spirit. That's what happened to my family and me, and all five of us are happier and healthier than ever before.

Honestly now when I look in the mirror that profound, deep frown line centered right between my eyes is faded and almost forever gone, and I know it will not ever come back. I won't allow it.

I've grown and blossomed into who I am today, a very different person from who I was even just a few short years ago.

I've opened up to "strangers" and learned to trust again. Being vulnerable isn't very comfortable, but I've come to discover that to cry together, we first need to celebrate each other.

We need to show up and walk the journey, even if it's a long, winding route. Even if it's painful to reach your destination, you will not be alone or lonely.

Your life is a journal waiting to be written in, filled with sticky notes and old pictures and a never-ending story that is uniquely yours.

People are here to help. Help you heal wounds, teach new ideas, share experiences, and listen and learn from each other.

As a group of like-minded moms, we are raising our children honestly, with love and determination, and with an open mind. Moms, with hearts overflowing with patience, and nurturing spirits to transform our child holistically. We now know, deep down in our core, that the unexpected by-product of this work will be a reduction of stress not only in your child and their overall well-being, but in you, and your family as well.

the ground, and I ended up resentful and bitter toward my child and family.

Luckily, implementing these self-care strategies strengthened my family ties and gave me a strength I never knew I had. Every day, I remind myself what this newfound change means to me, and that I am worth the time and energy required to allow myself this space for self-love. I no longer say, "I will get to it when...." I embrace it, nurture it and love it. I embrace me, nurture me, and love me.

Giving yourself permission to grow is mandatory as a woman and mom. Allowing time for self-care, especially when confronted with a daily onslaught of stress and anxiety, only makes sense. As a mom who takes the time to nurture your child, you know you need to create space and nurture yourself as well. If you don't do this, no one else will.

So, what do you do now?

- Nourish yourself from the inside out. Understand what foods reduce your stress and what adds to it. You make healthy food choices and understand the importance of vitamins and supplements.

- Spiritual support is key, so you relish soul time and seek it out daily. You deserve these peaceful moments where you practice your areas of quiet and optimism. Who knew the importance gained from mindfulness, gratitude and imagery?

- Cleaning your house of toxic relationships opens up a reservoir of new friends and communication. Your relationships will be much more meaningful, and you will grow closer as a family unit.

- Sleep habits are health habits, and with your new understanding of brain development and issues related to lack of sleep, you have a newfound respect for slumber.

- Natural healing methods will bring you closer to your child as you share in new techniques together. Yoga and exercise are fun and meaningful, especially when accompanied with aromatherapy and soothing baths. It's cool to share these together!

As this book comes to a close, I know that it is also a beginning. My hope is that as you delve into these five areas, you will be able to apply them to your life and see significant differences in your stress and anxiety levels.

Positive changes will occur for you, and there is no doubt about it, change will occur for your child and family, as well. Once you start, you'll find your practices are contagious and transforming.

Obviously, some areas might be easier for you than others. That's OK. Please know that there's help and support for you along this journey and you don't have to do this work alone.

There is power in numbers and support! It's a sign of strength to ask for help when you need it, and we all need help from time to time.

I would love to know how you are taking positive steps toward wellness, so email me as you head along with your journey. The ability to reduce your anxiety and transform your child at the same time is a gift to give yourself, your family, and your loving child.

And you, dear friend, deserve this and so much more!

Now is your time to embrace *your* self-care so that *you* can nurture and love *yourself* and expand *your* heart each and every day.

Join us today as you forge ahead with your spirited child and make positive, lifelong impacting changes toward wellness together.

ACKNOWLEDGMENTS

Greg, my oldest son, has said to me many times, "Mom, you should write a book." Just the thought of that made me chuckle, thinking, "A book?" I barely have time to write an email!" But I took his suggestion and tucked it away in my heart for another time and place. Years later, here I am writing a book.

Greg, I'm not sure this is what you had in mind, but thank you for your gentle prodding because without it the seed would not have been planted, and this book would not have blossomed. You've been a guiding, bright light from the moment you were born. I love you.

This work of love would not have been conceivable without my other two very different but astonishing and spirited children, Ryan and Devin. What I learned from your strength, dignity, and honesty throughout your lives, floods me with happiness and joy. I am so proud of you and honored and humbled to be your mom. I love you.

Parenting has been a non-stop roller coaster with crazy ups and downs and tight twists and turns. I wouldn't change a second of this glorious ride, but, most importantly, I'm grateful for the incredible learning experience that unfolded along the way.

And, without my kind and gentle husband, Steve, who guided me with love and insight, this adventure would not have even happened. I love you.

To my two sisters and brother: hopefully one day you will come to understand the strength and direct influence you have had on my life. My happiest childhood memories are of all of us together laughing on the front porch in Portland. I love you.

To my parents who taught me the meaning of love, family, and forgiveness. I know you are by my side every day keeping me safe.

To all the parents I've had the privilege to know while teaching in the public schools: your dedication and tireless quest to find the answers needed is impressive and so important. Your children gave me the knowledge and strength to deal with my own daughter's journey. Thank you for confiding in me and letting me be a small part of your journey.

To Angela and her team at Difference Press and especially Maggie McReynolds who made this entire process enjoyable and fun: thank you from the bottom of my heart.

To the Morgan James Publishing team: Special thanks to David Hancock, CEO & Founder for believing in me and my message. To my Author Relations Manager, Gayle West, thanks for making the process seamless and easy. Many more thanks to everyone else, but especially Jim Howard, Bethany Marshall, and Nickcole Watkins.

And finally to Todd Herman, my 90-Day Year Coach, who taught me how to persevere and never give up on my true dream and aspiration: you have no idea the impact you have had on this growth process. Thank you.

ABOUT THE AUTHOR

aureen Lake is a compassionate advocate for mothers who raise challenging children. She thoroughly enjoyed raising her three children and had a firsthand knowledge living a frenzied lifestyle of a mom who typically put herself last. Maureen has spent numerous years as a special education teacher and now a holistic health coach, but her passion rests with her desire to advocate for moms who want to create long-lasting positive change for themselves.

Her profound knowledge of creating an affirming lifestyle took her on a long and windy road to happiness. Maureen knows firsthand the roller coaster ride a mom goes through while striving to better herself and consequently her child. When her daughter, for the third time, was misdiag-

nosed she decided to pursue her lifelong love of writing to help other moms who have struggled right along with their child.

With a master's degree in special education and certification as a health coach, Maureen began her long career-teaching children with significant needs and later children with literacy challenges. She continued her career as a teacher of teachers and most recently coaching mothers in creating personal lifestyle changes.

Maureen lives in Colorado, and if she's not hiking with her dogs, you can find her indulging in Mexican food with her husband and three inspiring children.

Website: http://www.maureenlake.com

Email: maureen@maureenlake.com

Facebook: https://www.facebook.com/maureen.walshlake.9

Instagram: https://www.instagram.com/maureenclake

Pinterest: https://www.pinterest.com/maureenlake4

THANK YOU

Hey There!

Thank you so much for reading *Being Happy, Raising Happy*. Sharing my personal story isn't easy, just like I know what you are going through isn't easy either. I vacillated and debated for months about whether to write this book, but in the end, I felt compelled even if it could reach one mom struggling the way I was hurting for years throughout my path to wellness.

Your journey is a new beginning of a life-transforming difference for you and your child. I hope this book has provided you with support and the peace of mind you need, knowing many life-changing answers are on their way to you.

Please visit my website to download my free resource library full of helpful information, including stress-reducing recipes, valuable information about dyslexia & ADHD, quizzes, e-books, and educational information for you and especially for your spirited child.

Download the resource library here:

https://maureenlake.lpages.co/free-resources

Thank you for the opportunity to share my story with you. I look forward to hearing from you! Email me with any comments or concerns or if you'd like to work with me in the future.

Maureen Lake

Morgan James
Speakers Group

🔺 www.TheMorganJamesSpeakersGroup.com

We connect Morgan James published
authors with live and online events
and audiences who will benefit
from their expertise.

Morgan James makes all of our titles available
through the Library for All Charity Organization.

www.LibraryForAll.org

CPSIA information can be obtained
at www.ICGtesting.com
Printed in the USA
LVOW03s2055121017
552239LV00001B/1/P